ESSENTIAL MESSAGES FROM GOD'S SERVANTS

masterWork®

Lessons from

TEN SECRETS FOR A SUCCESSFUL FAMILY

by Adrian Rogers

TWELVE ORDINARY MEN

by John MacArthur

SUMMER 2005

Ross H. McLaren
Editor in Chief

Gena Rogers
Editor

Carolyn B. Gregory
Copy Editor

David Wilson
Graphic Designer

Melissa Finn
Lead Technical Specialist

John McClendon
Lead Adult Ministry Specialist

Mic Morrow
Adult Ministry Specialist

Send questions/comments to
Editor, *MasterWork*
One LifeWay Plaza
Nashville, TN 37234-0175
Or make comments on the web at
www.lifeway.com

Management Personnel

Bill Craig, *Director*
Leadership and Adult Publishing

Ron Brown and Jim Johnston,
Managing Directors
Leadership and Adult Publishing

David Francis, *Director*
Sunday School

Gary Hauk, *Director Publishing*
LifeWay Church Resources

ACKNOWLEDGMENTS.—We believe the Bible has God for its author; salvation for its end; and truth, without any mixture of error, for its matter and that all Scripture is totally true and trustworthy. The 2000 statement of *The Baptist Faith and Message* is our doctrinal guideline.

Lessons by Adrian Rogers are condensed from *Ten Secrets for a Successful Family* (Wheaton: Crossway Books, 1996). Used by permission of Good News Publishers.

Lessons by John MacArthur are condensed from *Twelve Ordinary Men* (Nashville: W Publishing Group, 2002). Used by permission of W Publishing Group and Thomas Nelson, Inc.

Unless otherwise indicated, all Scripture quotations in the lessons from *Ten Secrets for a Successful Family* are from the *King James Version*. This translation is available in a Holman Bible and can be ordered through LifeWay Christian Stores. Unless otherwise indicated, all Scripture quotations in the lessons from *Twelve Ordinary Men* are from the *New King James Version*. © 1979, 1980, 1982, 1984 by Thomas Nelson, Inc., Used by permission. Quotations in the "How to Become a Christian" article or those marked HCSB are taken from the *Holman Christian Standard Bible®*, copyright © 1999, 2000, 2001, 2002 by Holman Bible Publishers. Used by permission. This translation is available in a Holman Bible and can be ordered through LifeWay Christian Stores. Quotations marked AMP are from *The Amplified Bible, Old Testament*. Copyright © 1962, 1964 by Zondervan Publishing House. Used by permission. Quotations from *The Amplified New Testament* © The Lockman Foundation 1954, 1958, 1987. Used by permission. Verses marked *Living Bible* are taken from *The Living Bible*. Copyright © Tyndale House Publishers, Wheaton, Illinois, 1971. Used by permission. Passages marked NASB are from the *New American Standard Bible*. © The Lockman Foundation, 1960, 1962, 1963, 1968, 1971, 1972, 1973, 1975, 1977, 1995. Used by permission. This translation is available in a Holman Bible and can be ordered through Lifeway Christian Stores. Quotations marked NIV are from the Holy Bible, *New International Version*, copyright © 1973, 1978, 1984 by International Bible Society. This translation is available in a Holman Bible and can be ordered through Lifeway Christian Stores.

MasterWork: Essential Messages from God's Servants (ISSN 1542-703X) is published quarterly by LifeWay Christian Resources of the Southern Baptist Convention, One LifeWay Plaza, Nashville, Tennessee 37234; James T. Draper, Jr., President, and Ted Warren, Executive Vice-President. © Copyright 2005 LifeWay Christian Resources of the Southern Baptist Convention. All rights reserved. Single subscription to individual address, $26.35 per year. If you need help with an order, WRITE LifeWay Church Resources Customer Service, One LifeWay Plaza, Nashville, Tennessee 37234-0113; For subscriptions, FAX (615) 251-5818 or EMAIL *subscribe@lifeway.com*. For bulk shipments mailed quarterly to one address, FAX (615) 251-5933 or EMAIL *CustomerService@lifeway.com*. Order ONLINE at *www.lifeway.com*. Mail address changes to: *MasterWork*, One LifeWay Plaza, Nashville, TN 37234-0113.

Printed in the United States of America.

Cover photo credit: © Ercole de Roberti/
Getty Images/
The Bridgeman Art Library

table of contents

HOW TO BECOME A CHRISTIAN   2

Book One

ABOUT THE WRITER *Adrian Rogers*   4

INTRODUCING *Ten Secrets for a Successful Family*   5

Week of **June 5**	It Takes God to Make a Home	6
Week of **June 12**	One God Per Family	18
Week of **June 19**	The Name Above All Names	30
Week of **June 26**	Has the Nuclear Family Bombed?	42
Week of **July 3**	Don't Take What's Not Yours	54
Week of **July 10**	Truth and Satisfaction	66
Week of **July 17**	A Word of Encouragement	78

Book Two

ABOUT THE WRITER *John MacArthur*   90

INTRODUCING *Twelve Ordinary Men*   91

Week of **July 24**	The Apostle with the Foot-Shaped Mouth	92
Week of **July 31**	The Apostle of Small Things	106
Week of **August 7**	The Boanerges Brothers	116
Week of **August 14**	The Bean Counter & The Guileless One	128
Week of **August 21**	The Tax Collector & The Twin	140
Week of **August 28**	The Last Four	152

masterWork:
Essential Messages from God's Servants

• Designed for developing and maturing believers who desire to go deeper into the spiritual truths of God's Word.

• Ideal for many types of Bible study groups.

• A continuing series from leading Christian authors and their key messages.

• Based on LifeWay's well-known, interactive model for daily Bible study.

• The interspersed interactive personal learning activities **in bold type** are written by the writer identified on the Study Theme unit page.

• Teaching plans follow each lesson to help facilitators guide learners through lessons.

• Published quarterly.

ABOUT THE WRITERS

Adrian Rogers

Adrian Rogers has served for more than 30 years as pastor of the historic Bellevue Baptist Church of Memphis, Tennessee. This church is among the nation's largest churches with more than 28,000 members. He is founder of Love Worth Finding Ministries, an international syndicated television and radio ministry.

Dr. Rogers attended Stetson University and New Orleans Baptist Theological Seminary. Dr. Rogers and his wife, Joyce, have four children and nine grandchildren.

Dr. Rogers has been elected three times as president of the Southern Baptist Convention. He has been active in national leadership and has personally consulted and prayed with five presidents of the United States.

AMY SUMMERS wrote the teaching plans for these lessons. Amy is an experienced writer for LifeWay Bible study curriculum, a mother, and a Sunday School leader from Arden, North Carolina. She is a graduate of Baylor University and Southwestern Baptist Theological Seminary.

ABOUT THIS STUDY

What is your initial response to the introduction of this study?

❑ **I don't have children—what relevance does this study have for me?**
❑ **My children are grown and gone—what can I get out of this study?**
❑ **I've messed up so badly as a parent, it's too late for me.**
❑ **I can't wait to learn God's principles for a successful family.**

Spend time in prayer asking God to help you apply these principles to your life regardless of your family situation.

Ten Secrets for a Successful Family

𝒟o you want your family to be successful in the ways that count? to have a home where your children learn to love God and love others, and to turn that love into a living testimony for Christ? As much as you want this, God wants it even more. So much so that He gave parents a blueprint for building a spiritually successful family: the Ten Commandments.

All of the artillery of hell seems to be aimed at the nuclear family—humanism, relativism, materialism, hedonism. This material is written to give the family some weapons for the warfare.

A salesman was driving through the country trying to get to a certain city. He came to a fork in the road and stopped to question a farmer. "Does it make any difference which of these roads I take?" The farmer answered, "Not to me it doesn't."

Many of America's politicians, preachers, and teachers feel the same way. But when it comes to righteousness and truth, it makes a great deal of difference which road we take.

The next seven weeks of study will not only show you how to consistently, creatively, convincingly, and compellingly teach these 10 "liberating laws of life" but will lay out why it is so important to help write them on your children's hearts.

We *can* have homes that don't merely survive but thrive!

Adrian Rogers

It Takes God to Make a Home

Preparing the Way

Something terrible is happening in America. We are losing out spiritually in our homes, and the results of our loss are being felt in every corner of society. But God has a plan to give us successful homes. It is given to us in His Word and is communicated in the Ten Commandments, His perfect law. If we want to have homes that win, we can rediscover God's will as revealed in His Ten Commandments and transport His perfect plan for the home from the pages of Scripture right into our living rooms.

God has given us His unfailing and perfect plan for life, and we'll never have homes that are victorious and happy without them.

I realize that to some people the Ten Commandments may fall into the category of black-and-white television—okay for its time, but sort of out of date. My challenge to you is to hear and heed them afresh.

Before we home in on Exodus 20, I want to show you how vital this is and prepare the way by considering what many people believe to be the most important passage in all of the Old Testament—Deuteronomy 6:1-9. Here Moses tells us how we are to observe and teach God's Commandments.

SLOWLY read Deuteronomy 6:1-9 in your Bible. What do you think Moses desired for his people?

_____

What do you think God desires for your family?

_____

Week of JUNE 5

Something hit me like a hammer as I was pondering this passage in preparation for these studies. It clearly shows how God wants to communicate the Ten Commandments to His people. From father to child. It's that simple.

The Ten Commandments were not meant to be taught primarily in the public school, the halls of government, or the boardrooms of business. These places may be well and good, and the truth of God is certainly needed there, but they are not God's ideal plan. The primary setting for the communication of the Ten Commandments is the home.

The Book of Deuteronomy is Moses' farewell address to the people of Israel just before they entered the promised land. He was reminding the people of God's dealings with them and was preparing them to live in a way that would please God and guarantee them a future. Moses knew that God's answer to the chaos of pagan society was the family, and he wanted to strengthen and equip Israel's families to stand strong.

To set the context of Deuteronomy 6, we need to back up to chapter 5.

Scan Deuteronomy 5 in your Bible. What did Moses restate in this chapter?

_____

Notice verse 29, where Moses is speaking for God and says: "Oh that there were such an heart in them, that they would fear me, and keep all my commandments always, that it might be well with them, and *with their children for ever!*" (emphasis mine).

It will not be well with us and with our children if we do not make some radical changes and begin teaching the Ten Commandments in our homes.

Look at Deuteronomy 6:1-3 in the margin and underline who is to keep God's commands.

God says if you want your home and your nation to last, take these Commandments and hand them down from father to child. What a wonderful "winning streak" that would be for our homes—God's Commandments being handed down generation after generation.

"These are the commandments, the statutes, and the judgments, which the LORD your God commanded to teach you, that ye might do them in the land whither ye go to possess it: that thou mightest fear the LORD thy God, to keep all his statutes and his commandments, *which I command thee, thou, and thy son, and thy son's son, all the days of thy life; and that thy days may be prolonged.* Hear therefore, O Israel, and observe to do it; that it may be well with thee, and that ye may increase mightily, as the LORD God of thy fathers hath promised thee, in the land that floweth with milk and honey" (Deut. 6:1-3, emphasis mine).

7

day Two

Embracing God's Truth

> "Hear, O Israel: The LORD our God is one LORD: and thou shalt love the LORD thy God with all thine heart, and with all thy soul, and with all thy might. And these words, which I command thee this day, shall be in thine heart: and thou shalt teach them diligently unto thy children, and shalt talk of them when thou sittest in thine house, and when thou walkest by the way, and when thou liest down, and when thou risest up. And thou shalt bind them for a sign upon thine hand, and they shall be as frontlets between thine eyes. And thou shalt write them upon the posts of thy house, and on thy gates" (Deut 6:4-9).

I'm very concerned about the generation growing up today. Our youth have lost their hope. They have lost confidence in the future. It breaks my heart to see this happening.

But who are we listening to today? People who stand before the TV camera and confidently announce, "The cosmos is all there is."

Well, if this universe is all there is, the idea of a God must be obsolete. And if God is obsolete, His Commandments must be obsolete.

The Ten Commandments are not obsolete. They are absolute—absolutely true and absolutely necessary. And America's homes cannot hope to survive apart from the moral foundation they provide. Deuteronomy 6:4-9 (in the margin) tells us what God says fathers and mothers are to do with His Ten Commandments in the home.

Moses restated the Ten Commandments in Deuteronomy 5, and now God tells the people through Moses to teach these truths to their children.

We complain that the Ten Commandments can no longer be posted in public places. May I meddle a little? How many Christian parents know the Ten Commandments? How many of us have the Ten Commandments posted in our homes or in our minds?

In the margin, write as many of the Ten Commandments as you can from memory.

God told Moses, "Tell the people to put these laws upon the doorposts of their houses." And God says to fathers today, "It is your responsibility, not the government's or the school's responsibility, to teach these Commandments to your children." Dad, it's your job. I don't know where we got the idea that teaching God's Word and spiritual truth to children has been assigned to the school or is strictly women's work. The Bible always places the primary responsibility on fathers. We cannot punt the ball to our wives or the government or the school. It is up to us to see that the Ten Commandments are handed down to our children.

Week of JUNE 5

Psalm 127:4 says, "As arrows are in the hand of a mighty man; so are children of the youth." Fathers are God's mighty warriors to launch their children like arrows straight and true to the bull's-eye. If you have ever tried to bend and string a large bow like those used in archery competitions, you know how hard it is. It's even harder to pull the bow back and fire the arrow if you're not used to it. It takes strength and skill.

A father who wants to shoot straight as a warrior must be strong and skilled. Dads can't fire their "arrows" straight unless they are developing their own spiritual, mental, and emotional strength.

But fathers must also shape and sharpen their twigs into arrows. Children are not born arrows—they are born twigs. We are all twisted by sin from the womb. So the Bible tells parents to raise their sons and daughters in the "nurture and admonition of the Lord" (Eph. 6:4).

The warrior's aim must be true. He must keep the target in sight.

What do you desire for your children?
_____

What specific actions are you taking that are helping them aim toward God's target for their lives?
_____

If you aren't a parent, how are you influencing children in your extended family, church, or community?
_____

Once you sight the target, you need to fire the arrows. Arrows are not meant to be collected. They are to be projected. Our ultimate goal is to release our children spiritually and emotionally, not to try and keep them in the "quiver."

All of that is primarily the responsibility of the father. That's why I am thankful for the renewed attention being focused on fatherhood today. Amazingly, all of the studies and anecdotal evidence being gathered point to what the Bible has taught for centuries. If a husband and father is not the head of the family, the result can only be chaos. The father is God's person to lend stability and character and strength to the home.

Sadly, many dads today have forgotten their God-given responsibility to teach their sons and daughters about the Word of God, including the

"Unless the LORD builds a house,
its builders labor over it in vain;
unless the LORD watches over a city,
the watchman stays alert in vain.
In vain you get up early and stay up late,
eating food earned by hard work;
certainly He gives sleep to the one He loves.
Sons are indeed a heritage from the LORD,
children, a reward.
Like arrows in the hand of a warrior
are the sons born in one's youth.
Happy is the man who has filled his quiver with them.
Such men will never be put to shame
when they speak with their enemies at the city gate"
(Ps. 127, HCSB).

Ten Commandments. Our society is being devastated by the growing dilemma of negligent or absent fathers.

The great problem today is not delinquent kids but dropout dads and misguided moms who have failed to hand down God's truths from one generation to another. To keep from being that kind of parent and that kind of Christian, we need to mine this great passage in Deuteronomy 6 and see what God would have us learn.

Commit your family and your role in your family to God. Use Psalm 127 as the framework for your prayer.

day Three

Learning the Way

THE GREAT REVELATION: ONE LORD

"Hear, O Israel: The LORD our God is one LORD" (Deut. 6:4). There is just one God, one Jehovah, one Lord.

Everybody is going to believe in something or some kind of a god. But we're not just talking about the god of your choice here. Moses says the Lord God of Israel is unique. He is the only God. There is no other.

When your children (or peers) observe your life, what do they conclude is your god? Circle all that apply.

work   money/things   leisure activities
people   God   other: _____

THE GREAT RESPONSE: ONE LOVE

How should we respond to such a great revelation? "And thou shalt love the LORD thy God with all thine heart, and with all thy soul, and with all thy might" (v. 5).

The great revelation: one Lord. The great response: one love. And what kind of love? You are to love God with a sincere love—"with all thine

Week of JUNE 5

heart." Jesus spoke of people who "honoreth me with their lips; but their heart is far from me" (Matt. 15:8).

Do you know what your children need to see in your home? They need to see a sincere love for God. They need to see in you a burning, passionate, emotional sincerity when it comes to the things of God. Kids can spot a phony a mile away, and they know whether or not you love God with all your heart. It is the phoniness of parents, by and large, that turns kids off to the things of God.

You're also to love God with a selfless love—"with all thy soul" (v. 5). Your soul is your self, your being. What is Moses saying? To love God with your whole self, the totality of your being. Your whole self needs to be given to God. There needs to be no area in your life that is off-limits to God.

We could pretty well measure the spiritual love of men or women by looking at two books in their homes—their checkbooks and their date books—their bank accounts and their calendars. How you spend your money and your time says a lot about how selfless your love for God is.

Finally, we are commanded to love God with a strong love—"with all thy might." That means every inch, every ounce, every nerve, every sinew of your body. But Moses is not just talking here about physical strength. This includes emotional strength, financial strength, intellectual strength. You are to use it all in loving God.

On the lines below, mark the positions that best indicate your love for God.

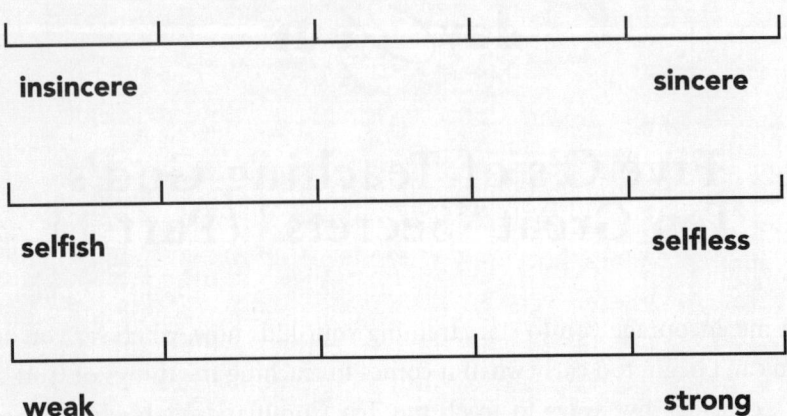

How do others (especially your children) perceive your love for God? Mark those positions with a star.

THE GREAT RESPONSIBILITY: ONE LAW

Because we have the great revelation of the one Lord who demands the great response of love, there is also the great responsibility—one law. One Lord, one love, one law.

Deuteronomy 6:6-7 gives us our great responsibility: "These words, which I command thee this day [not 10 suggestions or voluntary initiatives!], shall be in thine heart: and thou shalt teach them diligently unto thy children, and shalt talk of them when thou sittest in thine house, and when thou walkest by the way, and when thou liest down, and when thou risest up."

If you are from a broken home, or if you are a single parent trying to raise your children alone, don't be discouraged. You will find ideas to help you make up for an absent partner. My desire is to help and undergird.

There are powerful forces trying to shape and mold the mentality of today's youth. Many of them come home, go to their bedrooms, shut the door, and turn on a moral sewer called Music Television (MTV). Anybody who thinks kids aren't affected by what they see has rooms to rent upstairs. Why would a company pay one million dollars for a 30-second commercial during the Super Bowl if what people see doesn't affect them?

Our homes are to be law schools where God's Commandments are taught. The professors in this law school are primarily fathers, the students are the children, and class is already in session!

Five C's of Teaching God's Ten Great "Secrets" (Part 1)

Let me encourage you to start training your kids now, wherever you are. You can't begin too early when it comes to teaching the things of God. So let's consider five ways to teach the Ten Commandments, drawn from Deuteronomy 6:6-9.

Week of JUNE 5

TEACH THEM CONVINCINGLY

How do you teach the Ten Commandments in your home? Teach them convincingly. Notice in verse 6 that "these words" are to be in your heart first. If you don't believe something, if you don't practice it, just hang it up, because you'll never teach it.

> **Read Deuteronomy 32:45-47 in your Bible. Of what must you be utterly convinced if you're going to teach others God's commands?**

_____

Don't send your children to Sunday School or to the local Christian school and think you have done your duty. I tell the people in my church that it's not my responsibility to teach their children. Certainly I have a teaching responsibility as pastor, but my role is to support the teaching in the home, not to substitute for it. God's truth must be in your heart. You can't teach it convincingly to your children unless you're convinced.

TEACH THEM CONSISTENTLY

God's Word should be taught consistently or diligently. In verse 7 we read, "Thou shalt teach them diligently unto thy children."

> **Read Deuteronomy 6:7 again. When and where are parents to teach God's Word to their children?**

_____

Your teaching needs to be "precept upon precept; line upon line" (Isaiah 28:10). Build truth on top of truth; teach the Word over and over again. Don't say, "Well, I told them that. What's next?" Your children might need to hear that particular truth or exhortation again. Few, if any of us, learn everything we're supposed to the first time around.

Too many of us start and then quit, then start again and quit again. Be consistent in your teaching. You don't have to do it all in one day. The cumulative effect of "line upon line" teaching—spiritual compound interest—is wonderful.

How can parents apply the principles discussed in Days 4 and 5 to teach the Ten Commandments in the following situations?

You discover an unfamiliar sweater under your second grader's bed. She admits she took the sweater from a friend's house.

Your teenager's boss has scheduled him to work on Sunday.

As you're cleaning up your hard drive, you discover your sixth grader has been visiting illicit Internet sites.

Your three-year-old sees an amazing sight at the park and declares, "Oh my God!"

Your college-age daughter has focused all her attention on her boyfriend, neglecting academics, outside interests, and other relationships.

When you were growing up, what did your parents (or trusted adult) teach you repeatedly?

How did you respond? Check all that apply.
❏ rolled my eyes
❏ stomped away
❏ expressed gratitude
❏ followed their teaching when they weren't watching

What is your response today to that teaching?

day Five

Five C's of Teaching God's Ten Great "Secrets" (Part 2)

TEACH THEM CREATIVELY

You also need to teach God's Word creatively (v. 7). Use every means at your disposal—Bible reading, Bible stories, Bible games, Bible memory, Christian books and songs—to teach them.

The problem in many homes is that we suddenly get on a religion "jag" and say, "You kids are going to learn the Bible. So sit still while I instill." That's not the way God's Word is to be taught.

Charlie Jones, the great motivator, had a boy who was about to be 16. Charlie told him, "Son, when you get to be 16 you're going to want a car, and I am going to help you buy a car. But before then there are some books I want you to read and report on. I'll select the books. For every book you read you'll get $10 for your car fund."

Why did Charlie Jones do that? As he told his son, "If you read like a bum, you'll drive like a bum."

You say, "I don't believe in bribing kids." It's not a bribe. It's a reward. A bribe is an inducement to do evil. A reward is incentive for doing good. God rewards, and parents should reward too.

Week of JUNE 5

Read Proverbs 3:1-4 in your Bible. This ancient father taught his son if he followed God's teachings he would be rewarded with _____.

Check the rewards that would best inspire your children to consistently learn and obey God's Word.
- ❏ a date with Dad/Mom
- ❏ a hug
- ❏ "I'm so proud of you."
- ❏ watch a video together
- ❏ other:_____

TEACH THEM CONVERSATIONALLY

In verse 7 we're instructed to teach God's Word in the normal course of daily discourse. Take advantage of those times when a child's curiosity factor is high. If God's Word is a natural part of your daily conversation, your kids will catch on real quick. Remember, faith is caught as well as taught.

TEACH THEM CONSPICUOUSLY

Teach the Word conspicuously (vv. 8-9). The Jews took this so literally that they made little boxes called phylacteries, put the Shema in them, and tied them around their heads and on their wrists with a piece of leather.

Did God mean to do it that way? Perhaps He did. But what I think He meant was this: the Word "upon thine hand" reminds us that all we do is to be controlled by His Word. The Word "between thine eyes" reminds us that all we think is to be controlled by the Word of God.

Then Moses told God's people to write His Word on the doorposts of their houses. Again, the Jews did this by putting Scripture in a box or bag, called a *mezuzah,* and hanging it on their doorposts. Do whatever you can to make the Word of God evident in your home.

If you will teach God's Ten Commandments convincingly, consistently, creatively, conversationally, and conspicuously, your children will know that you really believe what you say you believe, and they'll believe it too!

Learn from the Master Teacher. Read at least two of the passages listed in the margin and identify how Jesus taught convincingly, consistently, creatively, conversationally, and conspicuously.

Matthew 23:1-12

Matthew 24:1-13

Mark 11:12-14,20-25

Luke 12:13-34

Luke 18:1-8

NOTES

To the Leader:

Each teaching plan offers two options for beginning the lesson. The first option is discussion oriented. The second option offers more creative or interactive ways to break the ice and create interest in the lesson. Feel free to combine and/or revise these ideas or let them inspire you to create your own opening. The goal is to set an atmosphere for learning by helping adults feel comfortable in the class yet challenged by the truth and eager to learn and be transformed by God's Word.

Before the Session:

1. Draw an archery target on a poster with a light-colored marker. Over the target, write the Ten Commandments with a black marker. (Get as artistic with this as your time and talent allow!)
2. Provide several translations of Ephesians 6:4. (Translations can be found at *www.biblegateway.com*.)
3. Prayerfully choose the steps you will use in your lesson plan.
4. You will have a challenge throughout this study to make the material applicable to those who do not have children. Ask God how you can help all learners apply the principles of this study to their lives. You can help learners explore how to implement these teachings in relationships with grandchildren, adult children, nieces or nephews, and children in your church and community.

During the Session:

1. Invite volunteers to share traditions or sayings that have been passed down in their families. Discuss the value of traditions. Ask: *Have you ever tried to break or begin a tradition? Why? How difficult was it?* Remark that it is difficult to break negative cycles of ungodliness in families and begin the positive cycle of godly obedience, but the success of families depends on it. This study will help learners implement secrets for a successful family. OR Invite learners to name television families from the past and present. Ask: *Which would you say are successful families? What distinguishes successful TV families from the dysfunctional ones?* Comment that the successful TV families usually followed basic rules of behavior that are plainly spelled out in the Ten Commandments.
2. Introduce Dr. Rogers' purpose for this study. Depending on the makeup of your class you may need to discuss: *What is the value of this study for people whose children are grown? For people who don't have children?*
3. Say: *Dr. Rogers asked who we are listening to these days. How would you answer that? What are these sources saying about God and humanity?*

Week of JUNE 5

How did Dr. Rogers say parents must respond to these falsehoods? Ask for a volunteer to read Deuteronomy 6:1-9. Ask what Moses desired for his people. Request that learners silently consider their desires for their children. Remark that parents who desire only worldly success, happiness, and popularity for their children may see their children make destructive lifestyle choices. Obedience to the Ten Commandments is always a positive desire we can have for children. Encourage the class to read aloud the Ten Commandments from the prepared poster. Ask whose responsibility it is to direct children toward the target of God's commands. Request that someone read Psalm 127:4. Discuss from Day 2 what Dr. Rogers said are requirements for a successful warrior in this battle for our children. Ask volunteers to read various translations of Ephesians 6:4. Ask, *What tools does this verse tell us to use to shape our children so they develop into straight-flying arrows?* Comment that parents must make the target clear so children know what is expected. Parents must also consistently hit the target themselves. (Be sure to acknowledge some parents fulfill their roles faithfully and their children still go astray, but generally most children will hit the target if that is where they are aimed.) Remark that this study is not designed to overwhelm parents but to equip them to fulfill their responsibilities.

4. Ask someone to identify three great truths parents must acknowledge if they are to guide their children to aim for God's will. [One Lord, one love, one law.] Ask: *What happens to the one love and one law when we don't adhere to the truth that there is only one Lord? Why?* Ask learners to identify the five ways Dr. Rogers said parents can be effective teachers of God's law. Read aloud Deuteronomy 32:47. Ask, *How can we demonstrate to our children that God's Word is our very life?* Allow parents to share what creative teaching resources and rewards have worked with their families. Encourage them to share how they teach consistently in the course of daily living and what conspicuous means they use to teach their children. Discuss how parents can apply Dr. Rogers' five principles to the case studies in the margin on page 14. (Feel free to alter these situations or make up your own to best fit the lives of your learners.)

5. Close in prayer, asking God to use this study to strengthen the families in your class and church.

NOTES

One God Per Family

The Priority Commandment

Last week we laid a foundation for our study of the Ten Commandments, considering from Deuteronomy 6 what God expected from His people in Moses' day and what He expects from us as His people today. We talked about how we are to keep God's commands and how we are to teach them to the next generation. Now I want to begin building the superstructure on that foundation.

The First Commandment rightly occupies the place of preeminence, the place of priority in the giving of the Commandments in Exodus 20. Obedience to this command should also occupy the place of priority in our lives today.

Verse 1 says, "God spake *all* these words" (my emphasis). The Ten Commandments came from the mouth of the Lord Himself. These are not any human being's ideas or suggestions.

Let's look at the First Commandment in the margin. There is only one Lord. All other so-called gods are merely the imaginations of men's minds or the deceptions of lying spirits.

This revelation of the one invisible, almighty God was, and still is, unique in history. The concept of a God who is pure spirit, who can neither be seen nor touched and who is wholly unlike us, was a radical departure from the pagan gods of antiquity.

THE GOD WHOM SCRIPTURE DECLARES

How do we know there is only one God? Number one, because Scripture declares the fact of God. The Bible presents the truth of God's existence as the first reality upon which everything else is built and depends.

> "I am the LORD thy God, which have brought thee out of the land of Egypt, out of the house of bondage. Thou shalt have no other gods before me" (Ex. 20:2-3).

Week of JUNE 12

THE GOD WHOM CREATION DISPLAYS

Not only do the Scriptures declare the fact of God. The creation displays the hand of God.

> **Read Psalm 19:1-3 and Romans 1:19-20 in your Bible and answer the following:**
>
> **What has God revealed in nature?** _____
>
> _____
>
> **Does anyone have an excuse for not believing in the one, true God?** ❏ Yes ❏ No ❏ Not Sure
> **Explain your answer.**
>
> _____

We talk about the laws of science by which the universe operates, but the fact is they're not laws of science at all. They are the laws of God that science has only discovered and described. Scientists are no more capable of creating those laws than Christopher Columbus was capable of creating North America.

Something is wrong in our nation, which was built on the fact that we are the creation of God and are therefore endowed with certain rights. Today we cannot teach our children in public school that they were created by God. For the heart and mind that is open and searching, every star and stone of creation reveals the glory and majesty of God.

THE GOD WHOM FAITH DISCOVERS

A third reason we know there is only one Lord is that we can discover the truth about Him by faith. Nobody has ever been argued into believing in God. Belief in God is not really an intellectual issue but a moral one.

Everybody is a believer, including the atheist. The atheist believes by faith that there is no God. I believe by faith that there is a God. The difference is with evidence. I have the external evidence of creation. And I have the internal evidence of the Holy Spirit in my heart.

God so created you that when your heart is right, it will respond to the fact of God the way a healthy eye responds to light or a healthy ear to sound.

Review the three reasons we can know there is only one God. Star the reason that is the most persuasive to you at this point in your life.

The B_____ tells me so.
C_____ tells me so.
My f_____ tells me so.

God's Commandment for Today

The First Commandment forbids us from putting any other god before the Lord. That means there is to be no rival to God, no rebuttal to God, and no refusal of God. The idea of "before me" is literally "before My face" or "in My sight."

This is still God's law for life today. It means if I am obedient, whatever He says, I will do. It means I will allow nothing to take the place of absolute priority in my life that He deserves and demands.

God's commands are not for our punishment, but for our welfare. Even though eight of the Ten Commandments are negative, there is a positive implied in each one.

State the First Commandment positively.

Thou shalt _____.

> "Whom shall he teach knowledge? and whom shall he make to understand doctrine? them that are weaned from the milk, and drawn from the breasts. For precept must be upon precept, precept upon precept; line upon line, line upon line; here a little, and there a little" (Isa. 28:9-10).

What God is saying is this: "Give Me first place in your life." He loves you, so every time God says, "Thou shalt not," He's really saying, "Don't harm yourself." And every time God says, "Thou shalt," He's saying, "Help yourself to happiness." We need to understand this principle. We must teach it to our children, and we have to begin early.

Read the words of the prophet Isaiah in the margin. That's how you do it. Not all at once, but little by little as the children are able to receive and understand it. The key here is consistency, faithfulness.

Week of **JUNE 12**

God's Word says, "Train up a child in the way he should go: and when he is old, he will not depart from it" (Prov. 22:6). Keep this great truth before you as we talk about obeying and teaching the Ten Commandments in our homes.

The best way to teach your children the truth of the First Commandment is to live it yourself. Your kids know whether you love God with all your heart. What they want to see is parents with such a love and reverence for God that they bring Him into every area of their lives and put Him first in everything. Kids want to see whether their parents love God enough to obey Him.

Think of the last negative thing you said to your child. Rephrase it here to make it a positive statement.

_____
_____
_____

Read John 14:15,21,23 and 15:10. What is the main way you can demonstrate to your children and others that you love God?

_____
_____

True love for God always translates into obedience to Him. So the First Commandment tells us *whom* to worship: the Lord God, the one and only true God. The Second Commandment tells us *how* to worship.

The *How* of Worship

We discussed earlier that the Ten Commandments apply primarily to the home. From the home, then, they impact other spheres such as school, government, and business. But the home is primary. So let's take a careful look at the second of these great principles for the home. Read Exodus 20:4-6 in the margin.

The First Commandment deals with the *who* of worship. The Second Commandment deals with the *how* of worship. The First Commandment forbids false gods. This Commandment forbids false worship. When the

"Thou shalt not make unto thee any graven image, or any likeness of any thing that is in heaven above, or that is in the earth beneath, or that is in the water under the earth: thou shalt not bow down thyself to them, nor serve them: for I the LORD thy God am a jealous God, visiting the iniquity of the fathers upon the children unto the third and fourth generation of them that hate me; and showing mercy unto thousands of them that love me, and keep my commandments" (Ex. 20:4-6).

Bible issues an injunction against false worship, then, just as surely as night follows day, the Bible is commanding true worship.

How would you describe the difference between false and true worship to your child or an unbelieving neighbor?

_____

_____

The best thing you can do for your children is to teach them how to worship the true God. What a privilege, what a responsibility it is to teach family worship, to learn how to worship God together as a family.

The Lord is the Master of the universe and of our lives, and He alone is worthy of our worship. The word *worship* means to ascribe worth to something. God is worth all that we have and are. The best thing you can do for your children is not a college education, not an inheritance in the bank, and not vitamin-enriched food. Those are all good. But the best thing you can do for your kids is to teach them to worship.

Read Psalm 135:15-18. Why is it imperative children learn to worship God and not false gods?

_____

The Bible teaches us that when we worship an idol, we become like that idol. First the family molds the idol, and then the idol molds the family. The good news is that this principle works positively too. When we worship God, we become like Him.

A Proper Conception of God—No Comparison

As parents and teachers, it is our duty and privilege to give our children a proper conception of God. If you have a warped concept of God, you're going to have warped worship and a warped life.

Idolatry is wrong because it gives a distorted or false picture of God. An idol is a material thing, and no idol can represent the invisible, spiritual God. Jesus said in John 4:24, "God is a Spirit." Spirit is His very essence.

Week of JUNE 12

No wonder, then, that Jesus went on to say, "They that worship him must worship him in spirit and in truth." What material thing could possibly represent spirit? There is nowhere where God is not, and no material thing can represent Him.

God Himself asked, "To whom then will ye liken me, or shall I be equal?" (Isa. 40:25). There's only one God. You can't compare Him to anything or anyone.

That's the reason some people have difficulty with the doctrine of the Trinity. That's all right. I wouldn't have any confidence in a God I could understand. Don't worry about trying to illustrate the Trinity. God says there is nothing like Him. Even if you could find something that was like God, you ought not worship it.

"I the Lord thy God am a jealous God" (Ex. 20:5). God has a monopoly on being God! God is not a part-time king. He is God! And He is "a jealous God." You have no right to worship anything or anybody but Him.

If you desire to dig deeper . . .

Read Isaiah 44:9-20 and list sad truths about those who worship false gods.

_____

_____

_____

_____

Read Deuteronomy 4:15-20 in your Bible. Draw a line matching the truths about worship to the verse that states that truth.

Nothing God or man has made is to be worshiped.	**Deuteronomy 4:16**
God isn't represented by material things.	**Deuteronomy 4:20**
Idol worship is corrupt worship.	**Deuteronomy 4:15**
Only God delivers and is worthy of worship.	**Deuteronomy 4:16-19**

Modern Idols

Yesterday we talked about giving our children a proper conception of God. We discussed that we can't compare God to anything or anyone. Today we will continue that discussion, focusing on modern idols.

Not all idolatry consists of sticks and stones. Most Americans today don't make graven images. Very few of us have some molten god that we worship.

Martin Luther has well said that whatever your heart clings to and relies on, that is your god. Anything you love more than God, anything you fear more than God, anything you serve more than God, anything you value more than God is your god.

Read Matthew 22:37-38. If you follow Jesus' teaching to the logical conclusion, what is the greatest sin? (underline one)

Adultery   Murder   Idolatry   Unbelief

What is the reason for your choice?

_____

Idolatry is the greatest sin for it is really a renunciation of the whole purpose of life. Why did God make us and set us in families? To love and worship Him. "For in him we live, and move, and have our being" (Acts 17:28). That is why we exist. You can have idols in your heart without making them with your hands.

As you read the remainder of Day 4, underline the idols worshiped in our society.

In America we have made gods of ourselves. "Me-ology" has replaced theology. Paul warned that in the last days men would be "lovers of their own selves" (2 Tim. 3:2), "whose God is their belly" (Phil. 3:19).

Some people have made a god of wealth. The evidence of this idolatry is easily seen. There are idolaters who will not unite with the church because they think membership may involve stewardship. The Bible says that covetous people will not inherit the kingdom of God (1 Cor. 6:10).

Some people even make a god of the family. You ought to love your family. You should adore your family. I do mine. You ought to sacrifice for your family. But you dare not make a god of your family. I'm not writing to help you learn to put your family above everything else. Quite the contrary. I want to help you learn how to put God first in your family.

Week of JUNE 12

The worst thing you could do would be to put your family first—because whatever is first is your god. My wife, Joyce, knows she is not number one in my life. I know I'm not number one in her life, and I'm glad I'm not. We both desire to put God first in our affections and in our worship.

Because Joyce loves God supremely, she is able to love me with a love she could not give me if I were number one. And by being number two in her life, I'm loved more than I could ever be if I were number one.

This is so important to teach and model before your children. They will be loved more if God is number one in your life than they could be if they were number one. Jesus Christ said, "He that loveth father or mother ... son or daughter more than me is not worthy of me" (Matt. 10:37).

That may sound harsh, but this is where we start to separate those who think the Ten Commandments are just nice little rules from those who desire a radical but exciting faith. Putting Him first doesn't mean you love your family any less. It really means you love them more.

Other Americans have made gods of pleasures—chiefly sports. Paul said that in the last days men would be "lovers of pleasures more than lovers of God" (2 Tim. 3:4). Our sports stadiums and palaces of pleasure are filled. Sunday has become "Fun-day." The new Sunday ritual is professional football or other athletic highs.

I'm not saying that you have to choose between God and pleasure. "At [His] right hand there are pleasures for evermore" (Ps. 16:11). But pleasures cannot come first. If you're a lover of pleasure more than a lover of God, you are an idolater.

We have too many idols and not enough heroes. We have sex idols and rock music idols and sports idols. But where are the heroes—the people worth admiring and emulating because of their character and integrity? One way you can help your children avoid this kind of idolatry is to help them find some real heroes and carefully examine their idols.

Before you expect your children to examine their idols, you must examine your own. Review the idols you underlined. In the margin, note specific ways your worship or rejection of these idols has undergirded or undermined your positive influence on your children or others.

A Persuasive Communication of God

Exodus 20:5 ends with a stern warning: "I the LORD thy God am a jealous God, visiting the iniquity of the fathers upon the children unto the third and fourth generation of them that hate me." God says that wrong worship is iniquity—sin.

Forget the idea that you can just choose however or whatever you want to worship without consequences. The iniquities of false worship show up in the children, grandchildren, and great-grandchildren of those who worship in a false way. That's the reason it is so tragic. God visits the iniquities of the fathers upon the children.

That doesn't mean God holds children guilty for their parents' sins. This is not talking about the guilt of the sin, but the tragic result of the sin. We see this in the natural realm. For example, when a mother-to-be is a user of crack cocaine, her baby is born with certain defects.

A GODLY HERITAGE

We're going to see the same thing happen to the children and grandchildren of America if we don't get back to the true worship of Almighty God. Nobody ever sins solo; we are linked together. There is no such thing as sin only hurting one person.

The hideous results of sin show up in the sinner's children. But there's a positive side to this matter of influencing our children. Let's go back to the Commandments in Exodus 20: "For I the LORD thy God am a jealous God … showing mercy unto thousands of them that love me, and keep my commandments" (vv. 5b-6).

Thank God for that promise. Thousands of our descendants will be blessed if you and I will faithfully teach our children how to worship the true God. I'm standing on Psalm 112:2.

Read Psalm 112:1-2 in the margin. Circle who will be blessed.

"Praise ye the LORD. Blessed is the man that feareth the LORD, that delighteth greatly in his commandments. His seed shall be mighty upon earth: the generation of the upright shall be blessed" (Ps. 112:1-2).

Week of JUNE 12

We can each look down the corridor of time and say, "Dear God, I want to start something growing. Please start a fire in me that will never stop burning. I want my influence to go on and on and on."

I love what Paul said to Timothy: "I call to remembrance the unfeigned faith that is in thee, which dwelt first in thy grandmother Lois, and thy mother Eunice; and I am persuaded that [it is] in thee also" (2 Tim. 1:5). This legacy of faith started with the grandmother, went down to the mother, and then was handed down to Timothy.

Are you living for your grandchildren? Are you living with your great-grandchildren in view? "The generation of the upright shall be blessed."

A Prayerful Celebration of God

Not only must there be a proper conception of God and a persuasive communication of God, but there must also be a prayerful celebration of God.

Your children must see that your love for God is the most important thing in your life. You can't teach your children to love and obey God with passion if your love is lukewarm.

It is imperative that we celebrate God in front of our children. This business of loving and serving God is not a matter of cold calculation. It's to be our passion, the consuming love of our hearts.

You cannot get someone else excited about something that makes you yawn. If you really believe God alone is worthy of your worship, and if you love and worship Him with all your heart, your children will catch the fever.

State specific ways your children can observe you love and worship God:

1. first thing in the morning _____

_____

2. as you're working around the house _____

_____

3. as you're relaxing _____

_____

4. on Sundays _____

NOTES

To the Leader:

Read again Martin Luther's comments about idolatry at the beginning of Day 4. Ask God to reveal to you those things you love, fear, or serve more than God—could those be perfection, fear, heartaches, your reputation as a Bible study leader? Don't attempt to teach your class about the perils of idolatry until you have repented of idolatry in your own heart. Once you have confessed, claim the promise of 1 John 1:9.

Before the Session:

1. Find a poster board and marker.
2. Not every weekly learning activity is referenced in the teaching plan. Prayerfully choose which activities and teaching steps you will incorporate into your lesson plan.

During the Session:

1. Ask: *When you were a child, what was the most important rule in your family? What happened when you broke this rule? Looking back, what do you think was the purpose for that rule?* OR Organize the class into small groups. Instruct each group to compile a list of laws they encountered on the way to Bible study. Discuss which laws they obeyed and which they ignored. Ask the groups to share their lists of laws. Ask: *Of all these laws, which would you say is the law you needed to give the greatest priority to obeying? Why?* FOR EITHER OPTION Comment that today you will study God's priority Commandment and explore how to instill that command in your children.

2. Request someone read Exodus 20:1. Ask what makes the Ten Commandments different from writings followed by world religions or cults. [God spoke them.] Ask, *How can we know God hasn't modified these words He spoke so long ago?* Ask a volunteer to read 1 Samuel 15:29.

3. Ask a volunteer to read the First Commandment in Exodus 20:3. Use the final activity of Day 1 to help the class discuss three ways people can know for certain there is only one God. Invite volunteers to share why any of those reasons are particularly persuasive to them right now. Complete the first activity of Day 1. Ask, *What opportunities and challenges do those truths present you as leaders of children?*

4. Invite learners to state the First Commandment as a "Thou shalt" instead of a "Thou shalt not" statement. Inquire, *If we truly believe and follow this command, what will our lives look like?* Read 1 John 5:2-3 to help answer that question. Guide the class to explore ways

Week of JUNE 12

parents can consistently impress the truth there is only one God to children in each developmental stage. Ask why Dr. Rogers asserted the First Commandment is the priority commandment.

5. Invite someone to read Exodus 20:4-6. Explain how this Second Commandment is closely related to the First. Read aloud "The best thing you can do for your children is to teach them to worship the true God." Ask if that has to be done with the family sitting quietly in the den for 30 minutes. Remind learners of Deuteronomy 6:7-8. Request that learners recall from Days 4 and 5 of Week 1 the five "c's" of teaching children God's law. Record them on the poster board. (Keep this for the remainder of the study as a guide for class discussions.) Lead the class to discuss how they can use these five "c's" to teach children to worship God.

6. Instruct learners to silently read Psalm 135:15-18. Ask why it is so important children learn to worship God. Lead the class to identify contemporary idols families worship and how those idols mold families. Ask, *If you become like what you worship, then what is the result of worshiping God?* Request that learners silently read Psalm 135:19-20 and insert their family name after "Oh house of...." Lead them to silently pray their house will learn to worship God.

7. Complete the Dig Deeper activity in the margin of page 23, or if time is growing short, present the results of your own study of Isaiah 44. Read aloud Isaiah 44:20. Explore how adults can help children see the lie in the lure of popularity or having the right car or clothes. Discuss how parents can use television, often the medium that most strongly promotes idolatry, to guide children to see the foolishness of worshiping idols.

8. Remark that Dr. Rogers said we have too many idols but not enough heroes and we must help children find real heroes. Ask: *Where can we find these real heroes? How can we be heroes for children?* Encourage learners to thank adults who work with children and youth in your church. Comment that what we do or don't do with children now will affect generations to follow. Ask how learners have observed the truth of Exodus 20:5-6.

9. Close by praying Psalm 112:1-2 for your class.

NOTES

The Name Above All Names

What's in a Name?

What's so important about a name? In Bible times, when a child was born the parents would pray over that child and give him or her a name that encompassed a prayer and a prophecy concerning that child.

That's the reason we see so many people in the Bible whose names match their character. Jesus is the perfect example. He came to be the Savior of the world, so the angel said to Joseph, "Thou shalt call his name JESUS: for he shall save his people from their sins" (Matt. 1:21). The name *Jesus* means "Jehovah saves." Names had great meaning in the Bible, so it's important that we understand what is conveyed in the name of Jehovah.

PERSONALITY IN THE NAME

The God we serve is a real Person, the self-named One, "the LORD thy God." When the word LORD is written in all capital and small capital letters, you are reading a translation of the Hebrew word *Jehovah* or *Yahweh*. This is the most personal name of God. He is saying to us, "I am Jehovah. I am a Person. Let Me introduce Myself to you."

By giving Himself names God is saying, "This is who I am. Learn My personality from My name." The name *Jehovah* speaks of the God who is a covenant-keeper.

POWER IN THE NAME

The Hebrew word *Elohim*, translated "thy God," speaks of a God who is the Mighty One. It is a plural word, because it speaks of the multiplicity of His strength and power. Jesus said in John 14:14, "If ye shall ask any thing in my name, I will do it."

> "Thou shalt not take the name of the LORD thy God in vain: for the LORD will not hold him guiltless that taketh his name in vain" (Ex. 20:7).

Week of JUNE 19

In the margin, list everything you anticipate doing today. Read Colossians 3:17 in your Bible. Star the activities on your list that the Bible commands you to do in the power of Jesus' name.

PROTECTION IN THE NAME

Not only is there personality and power in the name of the Lord—there is protection in His name. Proverbs 18:10 tells us, "The name of the Lord is a strong tower: the righteous runneth into it, and is safe."

Is Satan after you? Head for the name of Jesus. Take refuge in His name. When you breathe His holy name in prayer, it's like running into a strong tower for safety. You can see things from that tower that you couldn't see from any other place because there you have a wonderful perspective.

PROVISION IN THE NAME

There is also wonderful provision in the name of Jesus. We read in John 16:23 that our Lord said, "Whatsoever ye shall ask the Father in my name, he will give it you."

Anything you can sign Jesus' name to, you can have. But the key is asking in Jesus' name—not in your name or simply to fulfill your desires. But if Jesus wants you to have it, you can sign His name to the order slip, and God the Father will give it to you.

Check the requests you can be certain are asked in Jesus' name.
- ❑ Lord, please let him fall in love with me.
- ❑ Lord, bring my neighbor to salvation.
- ❑ Father, I'd sure like a black, all-wheel-drive vehicle.
- ❑ Lord, heal my loved one according to Your will.

PRAISE IN THE NAME

When you understand that there is personality, power, provision, and protection in the name of the Lord, you understand why praise ought to be offered in His name as well. The psalmist cries out, "O LORD our Lord, how excellent is thy name in all the earth!" (Psalm 8:1). "O magnify the LORD with me, and let us exalt his name together" (Psalm 34:3). What a privilege it is to praise God in the name of Jesus!

day Two

How Not to Take His Name

> "You shall not misuse the name of the LORD your God" (Ex. 20:7, HCSB).
>
> "You shall not use or repeat the name of the LORD your God in vain [that is, lightly or frivolously, in false affirmations or profanely]" (Ex. 20:7, The Amplified Bible).

We're not to take the name of the Lord our God "in vain."

What does that mean? (Hint: Read the translations of Exodus 20:7 in the margin.)

_____

The Hebrew word rendered "vain" means meaningless, empty of content. Can you imagine anything more out of touch with the character of God than to take His name in vain?

THE VANITY OF PROFANITY

One of the most ignorant things a person could ever do is profane the name of God. When you use God's name in profanity, it shows two things: an empty head and a wicked heart. Profanity reveals a feeble mind trying to express itself. But it also reveals a wicked heart truly expressing itself. "Out of the abundance of the heart the mouth speaketh," Jesus said in Matthew 12:34.

Profanity using the name of God is an insult flung into His face. It's so needless and unproductive. What does a person get when he takes God's name in vain? Only judgment.

You say, "Our family doesn't use that kind of language." That's wonderful. Do you permit secondhand swearing? I am referring to words such as *darn, dang, gosh,* and *jeez.*

"Oh," you say, "those are just euphemisms. They're just substitutes." Yes, they certainly are. *Gosh* is a substitute for the name God. *Jeez* is a substitute for the precious name of Jesus. And *darn* is a substitute for damn. Don't use even secondhand swearing or your kids might get the idea that profanity isn't all that bad.

One of these days God's going to put His arms around some of us and say, "Why did you take My name in vain? I'm your God—the God of the universe." What will we say then?

Week of JUNE 19

THE VANITY OF FRIVOLITY

This Commandment is not concerned primarily with swearing. That's as far as most of us go with it. But there's another way you can take God's name in vain, and that's by frivolity—using the name of God carelessly or lightly. Many of us do this much more than we use profanity.

It's all those little sayings, the flippant little phrases we use that include the holy name of God. How carelessly we may say, "God bless you" or "Oh, Lord." If we mean it, that's fine. But if it's just a little witticism or an offhand remark, that's something else.

It's as repugnant to God to take His name in frivolity as it is in profanity. So the best thing to teach your children is to never use God's name unless they're serious.

THE VANITY OF HYPOCRISY

There's a third way God's name is used in vanity, and that's in hypocrisy. I don't believe anything turns teenagers off more than hypocrisy in the home. When Mom and Dad do not live what they profess, it doesn't matter how active they are at church. The kids see right through them.

If you're going to live for God, live for God in your home. And when you take the name of Jesus on your lips, do not use that wonderful name in hypocrisy. Let your children know that you love Him.

Sometimes we even sing our hypocrisy when we come to church. We sing, "My Jesus, I love Thee, I know Thou art mine; for Thee all the follies of sin I resign." Do you sing that and yet harbor sin in your heart? "All to Jesus I surrender, all to Him I freely give." If you don't mean that when you sing it, you're not much different from a man who curses and swears. "The Lord will not hold him guiltless that taketh his name in vain."

Read Matthew 12:36 in your Bible. Have you spoken carelessly and misused God's name through: profanity? (even the substitutions) ❑ Yes ❑ No **frivolity?** ❑ Yes ❑ No **hypocrisy?** ❑ Yes ❑ No

What is the Lord leading you to do about your responses?

_____

How to Take His Name

In the negative there is a wonderful positive: taking God's name in victory. How do you take God's name in victory? I think the answer lies in Colossians 3:17—"Whatsoever ye do in word or deed, *do all in the name of the Lord Jesus*" (emphasis mine). That's taking His name in victory.

The last name given for God in the Bible is Jesus, the wonderful name that means "Jehovah saves." This is our Lord and Savior, Jesus Christ, the One who invites us to take His name on our lips in victory!

How can you help your kids learn to take God's name in victory? There are three things I tried to teach my children. I encourage you to teach these to your children as well.

1. Wear the Name

When we call ourselves Christians, we are wearing the very name of Christ. But to do that successfully, we've got to walk the walk.

When my children were little, I used to drive them to school. As they would get out of the car I would say to them, "Remember who you are—you're Christians. And you belong to Jesus Christ. You're not your own. You were bought with a price." I wanted my children to remember that they were wearing the name of Jesus when they went to school.

> **Read Colossians 1:9-10. Using this passage, write a prayer for your child or other loved one to wear the name of Jesus well.**
>
> _____
>
> _____

2. Share the Name

Teach your children to share the name. Malachi 3:16 is one of the grandest verses in the Bible. Read it in the margin.

"They that feared the LORD spake often one to another: and the LORD hearkened, and heard it, and a book of remembrance was written before him for them that feared the LORD, and that thought upon his name" (Mal. 3:16, emphasis mine).

Week of JUNE 19

Isn't that wonderful? God is so pleased when we even think on His name in victory that He has His angels record it in a book of remembrance. Imagine what it will do for your child's heart to know that he or she can make God so happy that He just has to stop and write it down!

When a person takes God's name in vain, it's because he doesn't fear the Lord. The greatest mark of character is the fear of the Lord. "The fear of the LORD is the beginning of knowledge" (Prov. 1:7). A nation is on its last legs when it no longer fears God.

If you want to teach your children something wonderful, teach them the names of God. What a wonderful study for your family devotions—the names of our God.

Read Psalm 9:10 in your Bible. What will happen when you teach your children the names of God?

_____

When we come to church, we need to talk about the Lord Jesus. The Bible calls us to "exalt his name together" (Ps. 34:3). When we come to church, we're also to be exhorting one another (Heb. 10:25). We talk about our Lord in song and in conversation. So many people are putting His name down, let's teach our children how to exalt God—to lift Him up. It's all part of sharing His name.

3. BEAR THE NAME

Read Acts 5:40-42 in your Bible. What do your children need to know may happen if they wear and share the name of Jesus?

_____

It's hard to believe, isn't it? His name is loved more than any other name on earth, but it's also hated more than any other. There is a concerted effort against the name of Jesus, but we must bear His name.

One day very soon we are going to see the King. On that great day, we will be so glad we learned to take God's name in victory and not in vain and that we taught our children to do the same.

Some names of God found in Scripture

God my Maker
God my Savior
Great and awesome God
Holy Father
Judge of all the earth
King of glory
Lord will Provide
My Comforter
My hiding place
Ancient of Days
Author of life
Spirit of counsel and power

day Four

God's Cure for Restlessness

> "Remember the sabbath day, to keep it holy. Six days shalt thou labor, and do all thy work: but the seventh day is the sabbath of the LORD thy God: in it thou shalt not do any work, thou, nor thy son, nor thy daughter, thy manservant, nor thy maidservant, nor thy cattle, nor thy stranger that is within thy gates: for in six days the LORD made heaven and earth, the sea, and all that in them is, and rested the seventh day: wherefore the LORD blessed the sabbath day, and hallowed it" (Ex. 20:8-11).

> "The heavens and the earth were finished, and all the host of them. And on the seventh day God ended his work which he had made; and he rested on the seventh day from all his work which he had made. And God blessed the seventh day, and sanctified it: because that in it he had rested from all his work which God created and made" (Gen. 2:1-3).

In this day of so many devices designed to save time, I've never seen so many hurried and restless people! If the computer, the calculator, the cellular phone, and all of these other technological wonders are supposed to save us time, why do we have so little time for the things that matter?

List devices designed to help people save time.

_____

What percentage of persons who use those gadgets would you say feel rushed and pressured?

0%   15%   50%   80%   99%

It seems with all we've accomplished, about all we have really added is speed and noise. We get there faster, but we don't know where we're going. And when we get there, we're out of breath.

A lot of people today are so frenetic, so pressured they don't know which way to go. And the place where the pressure and the restlessness often hit is in the home.

God has given us a cure for restlessness in the home, and therefore for peace outside the home. God has given us a day of rest. Many of us don't use it, and we don't really know much about it. But God gave a wonderful gift to us in the Fourth Commandment. Read Exodus 20:8-11 in the margin.

The very word *sabbath* means "rest." In fact, our English word is simply a transliteration of the Hebrew word for rest, *shabbat*. There are actually three primary rest days in the Bible. Let's deal with these one at a time.

CREATION REST

When God finished creating the world in six days, He rested. Moses recorded the event in Genesis 2:1-3 (in the margin).

God made the world in six days, and then He rested. Was He tired? Of course not. God never gets weary (see Isa. 40:28). He rested for the same

Week of JUNE 19

reason there are rests in music. It's not because the musicians are tired, but because they want to have a pause for emphasis and reflection—to rejoice in what has just gone before and to let it sink in.

But God's creation rest has been disturbed. What interrupted God's rest and put Him back to work? God's creation rest has been disturbed by sin, and until sin is fully and finally banished from His creation, there is work to do.

COVENANT REST

God gave His special covenant people a special day of rest—the seventh day, the day we call Saturday, the last day of the week (Ex. 31:13,16-17a).

The Old Testament sabbath, the seventh day of the week, was to be a sign of the covenant between God and the children of Israel. The sabbath was supposed to be a blessing to Israel. But they so contorted it that what was meant to be a blessing became a heavy burden.

Based on Mark 2:23-3:6, complete the following.

The Pharisees were angry because _____

_____

Jesus declared the original intent of the Sabbath by

_____

> "Speak thou also unto the children of Israel, saying, 'Verily my sabbaths ye shall keep: for it is a sign between me and you throughout your generations; that ye may know that I am the LORD that doth sanctify you.... Wherefore the children of Israel shall keep the sabbath, to observe the sabbath throughout their generations, for a perpetual covenant. It is a sign between me and the children of Israel for ever" (Ex. 31:13,16-17a).

CALVARY REST

Here's the third rest, the one that applies to you and me. This is the fulfillment of the sabbath for us, and this is how the Fourth Commandment applies to us in the church today.

Jesus did not come to earth to rest. He came to complete the work of redemption, and when He bowed His head on the cross He said, "It is finished" (John 19:30). His work was done.

When Jesus rose from the grave, we rose with Him because we are forgiven of all our sins. Praise God! We were dead, and now we're alive. We were in sin, and now we are forgiven.

I hope you're getting a sense of the privilege that is ours when it comes to this matter of rest. God's creation rest has been disturbed. The rest of the Old Testament sabbath became an unbearable burden for the people who were supposed to enjoy it. But in Christ our rest is complete. Hallelujah!

"Come unto me, all ye that labor and are heavy laden, and I will give you rest" (Matt. 11:28). What a glorious invitation. "I am your rest. I am now sitting at the right hand of the Father. My work is done. It is finished. Your sin-debt is paid in full." Jesus' finished work provides rest for you.

What do you need to do to receive the gift of Calvary rest? (check one)
❑ **come to Christ for the first time**
❑ **return to Christ after a long time away**
❑ **trust Christ and quit trying to do everything myself**
❑ **other:**_____

> "A Sabbath rest remains, therefore, for God's people. For the person who has entered His rest has rested from his own works, just as God did from His" (Heb. 4:9-10, HCSB).

> **If you desire to dig deeper ...**
>
> **Read about Sabbath-rest in Hebrews 3:7–4:11.**
>
> **Who can enjoy God's rest?**
>
> _____
>
> **Who is unable to enjoy God's rest?**
>
> _____
>
> **What do you think God's Sabbath-rest is?**
>
> _____

The Lord's Day

We celebrate the first day of the week as our day of rest and worship, not the seventh day. Why? Because Jesus came out of His grave on the first day of the week. Thus it is called "the Lord's day" in Revelation 1:10.

Sunday is not the last day of your weekend; it is the first day of the week, and you start it right by being in the house of God. The disciples met together to break bread, preach the Word, observe the Lord's Supper, and collect their offerings on the first day of the week.

Our Lord has fulfilled the Old Testament sabbath. He has transformed it into Calvary rest. The covenant sabbath speaks of the finished work of creation. The believer's Calvary rest speaks of the finished work of redemption. The first rest deals with natural life. Our rest with Christ deals with supernatural life. The first sabbath rest dealt with life in Adam. Our sabbath rest deals with life in Christ. The first commemorated the work of God's hands. Ours commemorates the work of God's heart. The first was a display of God's power. Ours is a display of His grace. The first was given to Israel. The second was given to the church. The first was a day of law. Ours is a day of love.

Is the Lord's day a holy day? Absolutely. It's holy because it's His. But it's a day of love and not legalism.

Week of JUNE 19

Pray: *Lord, how can I honor You today? How can I take this day and give You glory, reverence, and praise so at the end of the day I can say it was Your day?*

A Holy Day

Make the Lord's day a holy day. Make your worship on Sunday your highest priority—more important than your work on Monday. When you get up and go to worship on the Lord's day, you're saying, "God is important to me. My church is important to me. My brothers and sisters in Christ are important to me." What a wonderful message to instill in your children's hearts. If all of this is important to you, it will be important to them.

A Healthy Day

Make the Lord's day a time to be healthy. You should not only worship on this day, but rest as well. We need to teach our children industry. But we also need to teach them tranquility. Take the Lord's day and rest. Slow down. That's what He designed it to be. That's His will for you.

A Happy Day

Sunday ought to be the happiest day of the week. Why did the early church meet on Sunday? To celebrate the fact that Jesus came out of the grave on that day. After the resurrection of Jesus Christ, there's not a pessimistic or negative note in the New Testament. It's a celebration, a joy.

Make the Lord's day the happiest day of the week, and your children will look back on these days with happy memories.

Remember the sabbath day not as a day of legalism that God gave to the Jews so long ago, but as a day of liberty—Jesus has set us free to love and serve Him!

State specific things you can do to help your children (and yourself) know that Sunday is:
a holy day _____
a healthy day _____
a happy day _____

NOTES

To the Leader:

Reread the section entitled "Creation Rest" in Day 4. Take the risk of providing "rests" in the Bible study sessions—moments of silence that allow learners to consider a question or reflect on a profound statement. Pauses from speaking and teaching may promote the most powerful times of learning and transformation.

Before the Session:
1. Make certain the Ten Commandments poster you made for Week 1 and the 5 "c's" poster you made in Week 2 are still displayed.
2. Prayerfully prepare your teaching plan using the learning activities and teaching steps that best fit the needs and interests of your class. Feel free to do your own commentary study of the Ten Commandments to add more information, but always strive to help your learners discover truths for themselves rather than just feed them information.

During the Session:
1. Invite learners to share why their parents gave them their name, how they received a nickname, or why they chose a particular name for their child. OR Direct learners to call out the first word that comes to mind when you call out several names. Include names such as Benedict Arnold, George Washington, Judas Iscariot, Hank Aaron, Abraham Lincoln, Adolf Hitler, Bill Gates, Osama Bin Laden. (You might want to add names of church staff or class members if you're certain the person won't be insulted or embarrassed.)
2. Ask what is so important about a name. Explain the significance of names in biblical times. You can discuss this issue deeper by looking at the original names and name changes of Abraham in Genesis 17:3-5 (Abram—"exalted father;" Abraham—"father of many") and Jacob in Genesis 25:24-26 and 32:24-28 (Jacob—"he grasps the heel" or "he deceives;" Israel—"he struggles with God"). Remark that if human names are important, then God's name is extremely significant. Ask learners to share reasons they tell someone their name. Ask a volunteer to read Exodus 3:13-14. Ask: *Why did God tell Moses His name? What does the name God revealed to Moses tell you about His personality?* Ask how knowing a person's name, such as the CEO of a company, imparts power. Ask how knowing God's name makes

Week of JUNE 19

godly power available. Allow volunteers to share how they have experienced protection and provision in God's name. Inquire, *What should result from knowing God through His name?* [Praise His name.]

3. Ask, *What is the opposite of praising God's name?* Request that someone read the Third Commandment from the margin in Day 1. Request learners silently read the translations of Exodus 20:7 in the margin of Day 2 and ask how those help them understand the commandment more fully. Ask: *How might someone misuse your name? How would that reflect on your reputation or character?* Lead a discussion about how God's name is misused today and how that reflects on His character. Read aloud Matthew 12:36 and urge learners to silently consider the final activity in Day 2. Read aloud Matthew 12:34b and ask, *If we misuse God's name, what does that say about our hearts?* Encourage learners to start with their heart attitude about God if they desire to clean up their speech about God. Lead a discussion about how parents can help their children use God's name properly, using the material from Day 3 and the 5 "c's" of teaching you recorded on the poster last week (from Week 1, Days 4 and 5).

4. Discuss the first activity of Day 4. Ask: *What has all this hurry done to families and their acknowledgment of the one true God? What is God's cure for this mad rush?* Ask someone to read the Fourth Commandment. Discuss the background for this command using the material under "Creation Rest" in Day 4. Comment that the Jews took this gift of rest and converted it into an unbearable burden. Discuss the activity under "Covenant Rest." Ask how the Pharisees responded to Jesus' interpretation of this command. Request that someone read Matthew 15:6. Discuss how present-day believers might nullify or revoke the gift of this commandment for the sake of their own Sunday traditions. Help learners explore the meaning of "Calvary rest" using the information in Day 4 and the margin activity on page 38.

5. Ask: *How can we celebrate the original intent of this command without making it a legalistic list of good and bad activities for Sundays?* Discuss the final activity of Day 5.

6. Close in prayer, incorporating the prayer activity in Day 5 in your petition.

NOTES

Has the Nuclear Family Bombed?

> "Honor thy father and thy mother: that thy days may be long upon the land which the LORD thy God giveth thee" (Ex. 20:12).

Becoming Worthy of Honor (Part 1)

I want to turn the Fifth Commandment around and think with you about being the kind of fathers and mothers your children can honor. Why? I can't teach your children to honor you. That's your responsibility.

Don't get the idea that you have to be a perfect parent to live up to the Fifth Commandment. You're not a perfect parent, and your children are not perfect children. You also cannot guarantee how your children will turn out. Some people have almost put themselves in an early grave because they've had a wayward child. They prayed, sacrificed, loved, and taught, and their child made bad choices anyway.

God gave your child a will. He had two children of His own in the garden of Eden, and they didn't do so hot. Why? Because God gave them a will. That's the reason I believe you ought not have goals for your children. I don't have goals for my children and grandchildren. I have desires for them, but I can't control what they do and become, and I wouldn't want to. I do have goals for myself because I can control myself, by God's grace.

My desire is for godly children and grandchildren. My goal is to be a godly father and grandfather, worthy of their honor.

What I'm trying to do is to relieve you from the burden of perfectionism that says if your child fails, it's your fault—it's because you did something wrong or didn't do something right. It's only by the grace of God that any of us survive parenthood.

Are you real? Are you genuine? If your children know you're real, and they watch you handle your failures and problems, they will learn far more than they'll learn from any phony perfectionism.

Week of JUNE 26

I want to give you five simple and very achievable ways you can not only gain your children's honor, but prepare them to live successfully for the Lord and in turn become honor-worthy parents themselves.

1. BY LOVING THEM

The first way you can become a father or mother worthy of being honored is by loving your children. Real parental love is not giving your children what they want but what they need.

One way to love your children is by *touching* them.

Read Luke 15:20 in your Bible. What did the father of the prodigal son do when his son came home?

_____

What a beautiful picture of fatherly love! That's the way a father is supposed to love.

Hug your kids often. Hug them affectionately. Hug them supportively. Hug them tenderly. Hug them playfully, even when that teenaged boy says, "Aw, Mom" and tries to pull away. Inside, he still wants you to hug him.

Don't stop once they reach adolescence. They long for your affirmation and appreciation. They will love you for it. More importantly, they will emulate your example when God gives them their own families. Love your children by touching them.

You can also love your kids by *blessing* them. The Bible teaches that we parents have an awesome weapon called a blessing. We can bless our kids in such an incredible way. There are few things in life that will give your children more peace and confidence than the gift of your blessing. My father blessed me, and I praise God for it.

You also bless your children when you take their joys and sorrows seriously. Little children hurt. Don't laugh at their pain when the doll is broken or the pet dies. Children's pain in their world is just as real as your pain.

Older children need your blessing in a different way. They need to know that you believe in them and have high hopes for their future. They need to know that as they dream and hope and plan, they have your blessing to go for it, to be all God wants them to be.

Another way to love your children is by *listening* to them. We adults think we listen, but all too often the kids barely get a full sentence out of

"Listen, my son, and be wise; keep your mind on the right course. Don't associate with those who drink too much wine, or with those who gorge themselves on meat" (Prov. 23:19-20, HCSB).

"A righteous man is cautious in friendship, but the way of the wicked leads them astray" (Prov. 12:26, NIV).

"My son, keep your father's command, and don't reject your mother's teaching. …They will protect you from an evil woman, from the flattering tongue of a stranger. Don't lust in your heart for her beauty or let her captivate you with her eyelashes" (Prov. 6:20,24-25, HCSB).

"I will give them a heart to know Me, that I am the LORD. They will be My people, and I will be their God because they will return to Me with all their heart" (Jer. 24:7, HCSB).

"For God has not given us a spirit of fearfulness, but one of power, love, and sound judgment" (2 Tim. 1:7, HCSB).

their mouths before we jump in with our advice. One of the finest forms of communication is saying nothing. Sit down and listen, and you'll communicate your love without having to say a word.

Finally, love your children with your *prayers*. Pray for them, pray for them again, and then pray for them some more. The most loving thing you can do is to carry your children to the throne of grace in prayer.

Use the Scriptures in the margin to voice powerful prayers for your children (or loved one). Claim a verse a week for your child; write it on an index card and display it in a prominent place so you can pray consistently for your child.

day Two

Becoming Worthy of Honor (Part 2)

Yesterday we talked about ways to love our children. Today we will look at the other four ways to gain our children's honor.

2. BY LIFTING THEM

A second way to gain your children's honor is by lifting them—building them up—through wise encouragement.

Colossians 3:21 is a key verse here: "Fathers, provoke not your children to anger, lest they be discouraged." Wise encouragement is better than lavish praise. When you catch them doing something right, let them know through your encouragement that you believe in them. Let your speech affirm them.

What is the difference between encouragement and praise? Praise says, "Great! You cleaned up your room." In contrast, encouragement says, "It's great that your room got cleaned up. I really appreciate your effort." Encouragement focuses primarily on the child doing the achieving, not on the achievement itself. It says, "Thank you. I'm so grateful for you."

I'm not saying there's anything wrong with praise. But I do believe encouragement is twice as strong because it shines the spotlight where it needs to be.

Week of JUNE 26

3. BY LIMITING THEM
A third way to become the kind of parents children can honor is by setting healthy limits for them. It takes firm restrictions to set children free. It is your responsibility to liberate your kids by limiting them.

> **Read 1 Samuel 3:11-13. Why did the Lord bring judgment on Eli and his family?**
>
> _____
>
> _____

"I have told him that I will judge his house for ever for the iniquity which he knoweth; because his sons made themselves vile, and he restrained them not" (1 Sam. 3:13).

Eli didn't set any limits for his boys, and it cost all of them dearly. Your child needs to have limits. When God put Adam and Eve in the garden, He gave them all they needed, but He also gave them limits. There was one thing they were not to do. Even though they did it anyway, God's example of setting limits is a positive one.

Our limits have to be drawn in love. But if you set firm limits, and if your children know you love them, when they push against the rules and those rules don't move, they have security. We all inwardly desire limits.

Society in general looks upon rule-setting as something bad, but it's one of the most valuable things a parent can do. If our children don't learn to live within limits now, when will they?

4. BY LEADING THEM
How can you be an honorable parent? By leading your children. By showing them how to do right rather than just telling them how to do right. We are to train our children in the way they should go (see Prov. 22:6). To teach without training is to fail in the task.

What kind of character do you want your children to develop and display? You've got to lead them in developing character. Show them by example what a man or woman of character looks like.

Look at this list for a moment: contentment, courage, courtesy, discernment, fairness, friendliness, generosity, gentleness, helpfulness, honesty, humility, kindness, obedience, orderliness, patience, persistence, self-control, tactfulness, thankfulness, thriftiness, wisdom. Who is teaching these qualities of character? Mom and Dad, it needs to be you.

5. By Laughing with Them

Do you want to be an honorable parent? Lighten up. Learn how to laugh. Make your home a place of joy and laughter. You need to learn how to laugh because serious situations often call for a lot of laughter.

Human beings are the only creatures of God who can laugh, weep, and blush. Our emotions are part of what it means to be made in God's image. As part of that, laughter is God's gift to us. He is saying that laughter is a blessing. Let your kids see you laugh at yourself, at your mistakes.

Make your home the happiest place on the block, and your children will rise up and bless you for it. Let your house ring with laughter. Let your children see you laugh in times of trouble, because it means that God is over it all.

Read Genesis 21:6-7; Job 8:21; Psalm 126:1-2; and Luke 6:21 in your Bible. Do you notice a pattern?

Each instance of laughter followed a time of

_____.

How can you use that truth to bless your children?

_____

Families That Choose Life

Life is God's wonderful gift to us. Since He is the author of life, He also gets to set the rules by which it is to be lived. I believe God established the sanctity of human life the moment He created Adam and Eve in His image.

Read Genesis 4:8-12 in your Bible. Did God hold Cain accountable for the murder of his brother BEFORE or AFTER He gave the Sixth Commandment? (circle)

Week of JUNE 26

Later, after the Flood, God gave this command to Noah: "Whoso sheddeth man's blood, by man shall his blood be shed: for in the image of God made he man" (Gen. 9:6). This verse clearly prohibits murder. That's important because this is also the intent of the Sixth Commandment. This is a very specific command, not just a general prohibition against all forms of life-taking. The word translated "kill" is actually a rather rare Hebrew word that means "murder."

So, for instance, those who break into laboratories to set experimental mice or rats free or smash the lobster tank at a restaurant to free the lobster on the premise "Thou shalt not kill" are about as far off the mark as they can get. This Commandment is a prohibition against the willful taking of human life.

More serious is the argument that the Sixth Commandment forbids capital punishment. Those who hold this position argue that the death penalty is merely state-sanctioned murder that only multiplies the violence. That argument finds no support in Scripture. The very fact that human life is sanctified in God's sight makes the deliberate taking of a life in murder the most heinous act possible. In fact, the Bible is very clear and very specific about the penalty for violating this Commandment.

Genesis 9:6 spells out for all generations the penalty for murder: the forfeiture of the murderer's own life. Later God made capital punishment a permanent part of Israel's law code. In the very next chapter after the giving of the Ten Commandments, Moses records God's punishment for deliberate, premeditated murder. It is death at the hands of the duly appointed authorities (see Ex. 21:12,14).

The purpose here is not to debate capital punishment. But it's important that you understand God's intent behind His Commandments, because our society is moving further and further away from the bedrock biblical teaching of the sanctity of human life.

You need to teach your children the value of this thing called life and the seriousness of taking another life. Tomorrow I want to develop for you the positive side of the Sixth Commandment. I want to help you teach your children to choose life.

"Thou shalt not kill" (Ex. 20:13).

Reword Exodus 20:13 into a positive command.

Thou shalt _____.

Name specific instances when you can impress this positive view of life upon your children.

_____

The Great Life-Giver

The key verse in the New Testament that helps us understand the Sixth Commandment is John 10:10.

> "The thief cometh not, but for to steal, and to kill, and to destroy: I am come that they might have life, and that they might have it more abundantly" (John 10:10).

Read John 10:10 in the margin and complete the following:
The thief is _____ and his purpose is to _____.
Jesus' purpose is to _____.

Satan is the great life-destroyer. Jesus is the Great Life-Giver. Jesus Christ gives us three kinds of life.

1. Physical Life

Jesus has given us physical life. The Bible says that all things were made by Him (John 1:3; Col. 1:16), and that includes us.

And how did He make you? Genesis 2:7 says it so clearly: "The LORD God formed man of the dust of the ground, and breathed into his nostrils the breath of life; and man became a living soul." Here is a truth you need to teach over and over again to your children, because they're not going to get it in the public schools.

Evolution is a bias against Almighty God. And because it is the dominant theory of origins in our culture and in our educational system, we need to teach our children that Jesus Christ is the author of physical life.

Read Psalm 139:13-16. Using the truths in these verses, write a note to your children, assuring them their physical life is a beautiful gift from God.

If you don't have children, write a note to a friend, explaining why abortion is a violation of the Sixth Commandment. (Consider actually giving this note to your children or friend.)

2. SPIRITUAL LIFE

Jesus also gives us spiritual life. He said, "I am the way, the truth, and the life; no man cometh unto the Father, but by me" (John 14:6).

When Jesus said "I am the way," He was saying, "Without Me there is no going." When He said, "I am the truth," He was saying, "Without Me there is no knowing." When He said, "I am the life," He was saying, "Without Me there is no growing."

Christians are not just nice people who are trying to do better. They are not just those who have accepted some doctrinal creed or code of conduct. They are new creatures, having been supernaturally regenerated and transformed by Jesus Christ, who sends His Spirit into their hearts and gives them supernatural life.

3. ETERNAL LIFE

This same Jesus who gives us physical and spiritual life also gives us eternal life. In John 10:27-28 Jesus says this concerning those who believe in Him: "My sheep hear my voice, and I know them, and they follow me: and I give unto them eternal life; and they shall never perish."

Eternal life speaks of the quality of life as well as the quantity of life. Jesus adds years to the life and life to the years.

The Life-Destroyer

Satan comes to steal, kill, and destroy. In John 8:44 Jesus was speaking to the Pharisees, and He told them, "Ye are of your father the devil, and the lusts of your father ye will do: he was a murderer from the beginning."

"I have set before thee this day life and good, and death and evil; in that I command thee this day to love the LORD thy God, to walk in his ways, and to keep his commandments, and his statutes, and his judgments, that thou mayest live and multiply: and the LORD thy God shall bless thee in the land whither thou goest to possess it. But if thine heart turn away, so that thou wilt not hear, but shalt be drawn away, and worship other gods, and serve them; I denounce unto you this day, that ye shall surely perish, and that ye shall not prolong your days upon the land, whither thou passest over Jordan to go to possess it. I call heaven and earth to record this day against you, that I have set before you life and death, blessing and cursing: therefore choose life, that both thou and thy seed may live: that thou mayest love the LORD thy God, and that thou mayest obey his voice, and that thou mayest cleave unto him: for he is thy life, and the length of thy days: that thou mayest dwell in the land which the LORD sware unto thy fathers, to Abraham, to Isaac, and to Jacob, to give them" (Deut. 30:15-20).

Since Satan is a murderer and the Sixth Commandment says, "Thou shalt not kill," this is another way of saying that we must reject Satan.

In your opinion, what does Satan want to kill?

_____

Satan wants to bring death to youth, death to purity, death to joy, death to happiness. He wants to bring physical death, spiritual death, and eternal death. He wants to make your life not abundant, but miserable.

Why does Satan hate life? Because he hates man. And why does he hate man? Because man is made in the image of God, and Satan hates God. But he cannot get at God, so he tries to get at you and your family instead. Let's learn how to protect ourselves and our families against Satan, the destroyer of life.

PROTECTING LIFE

When the children of Israel were facing their inheritance, the promised land, Moses called them together and gave them the words in Deuteronomy 30:15-20.

**As you read Deuteronomy 30:15-20 in the margin underline the word *life* each time it appears.
Now go back and look at each statement associated with the word *life*. What does it teach you about life?**

_____

The Lord is our life. What a great statement! It's not that He only gives life. He *is* life. We're talking about helping our children choose life instead of death.

The family is meant to protect physical life. From what? First of all, from intentional killing, homicide, just as the Sixth Commandment says. The home was meant to be a place of safety. But many homes are so violent today that the young people in them are afraid to be at home, so they hang out on the streets.

The family is also designed to protect its members from the crime of suicide. I've been alarmed at the rate of teenage suicide. What a grievous

Week of JUNE 26

thing it is for anybody to take his or her own life, especially a child or youth whose life Satan has succeeded in destroying.

Our lives belong to God because He is the giver of life. Teach your kids that we should never take into our own hands matters that only God is wise enough, strong enough, and good enough to handle. Jesus will give us grace to face whatever comes our way. Help them hide 1 Corinthians 10:13 in their hearts.

A third way that our families need to protect life is by protecting the unborn from the crime of abortion. If you want your children to grow up to be people who choose and hallow life and in so doing obey the Sixth Commandment, you can't do any better than to teach them to choose and protect life while it is in the womb. If the Sixth Commandment means anything, it means we must protect the unborn against the heinous sin of abortion.

Cruelty too is a way of killing people. Some children have put wrinkles in their parents' brows and sent them to an early grave by their heartlessness. Cruelty may take years to kill its victim, but it's very effective.

According to Matthew 5:21-22, how did Jesus say we can break the spirit of the Sixth Commandment?

_____

Do you hate somebody? Is your heart a headquarters for malice? Make your home a place of love, forgiveness, and happiness, not a refuge for bitterness. You'll be obeying God, and you'll help your children see the value of choosing spiritual life.

The best thing you can do to protect your family's eternal life is to lead your children to a saving knowledge of Jesus Christ. Dear Christian parent, help your family choose life. Determine that you will not go to heaven without taking all of your children with you. Bring them to Jesus, the Great Life-Giver. Satan deals in death, but Jesus has come that we might have abundant and eternal life.

> "You have heard that it was said to our ancestors, Do not murder, and whoever murders will be subject to judgment. But I tell you, everyone who is angry with his brother will be subject to judgment. And whoever says to his brother, 'Fool!' will be subject to the Sanhedrin. But whoever says, 'You moron!' will be subject to hellfire" (Matt. 5:21-22).

Amy SUMMERS

NOTES

To the Leader:

With your class in mind, reread the section "By Loving Them" in Day 1. How can you touch each class member appropriately to show them love—a hug, firm handshake, gentle squeeze on the shoulder? Ask God to show you how to bless each person who walks into your classroom. Evaluate your listening skills—do you dominate the class session or really listen as members tackle the truths of Scripture? Finally, do you pray for each class member by name? Ask the Lord to give you a Scripture to claim for each learner. You have been given the marvelous privilege of leading this group of adults—love them!

Before the Session:

1. Make certain the Ten Commandments poster you made for Week 1 and the 5 "c's" poster you made in Week 2 are still displayed.
2. Study 1 Samuel 2:12–4:18.

During the Session:

1. Ask: *What are the greatest challenges children face today? What are the greatest resources children have to help them face those challenges? On a scale of 1 to 10, with 1 being not important and 10 being extremely important, how important is it for children to have respectful, obedient relationships with their parents if they are to rise above today's challenges? Why?* Comment that today you'll discover how to be the kind of parent children can honor. OR Read aloud Ephesians 6:1-3. Ask, *If you were writing a lesson for children based on these verses, what specific things would you tell them to do to obey and honor their parents?* Read aloud Ephesians 6:4. Ask, *If you were a child writing a lesson for parents based on this verse, what specific things would you tell parents to do to not exasperate you?*

2. Comment that no matter how much children struggle to be free of all parental control, they are really asking parents to be worthy of honor by doing five things. Request learners refer to Day 1 and state the first thing children are begging parents to do for them. Ask: *What does loving our children NOT mean? What specific things does Dr. Rogers say we can do to let our children know we love them?* To explore the concept of blessing, ask learners if they have ever commented that someone blessed them. Ask: *What did you mean by that? What specific things did that person do to cause you to feel blessed? What does it mean to bless our children? What specific things can we do to bless them?* Lead the class to discuss how each of the Scriptures in the margin on page 44 can be voiced as prayers for children. Encourage learners to claim Scripture in prayers for their children and to let their children know they're praying for them.

Week of JUNE 26

3. Ask learners to recall from Day 2 the second thing Dr. Rogers said parents can do to gain their children's honor. Help them explore the difference between praise and encouragement by guiding them to rephrase the following praises into statements of encouragement: "Those are really good grades." "That's a nice outfit." "You're the best musician in that band/player on that team." "That was a nice thing to do."
4. Ask why children inwardly cry out for limits even when they outwardly fight against restrictions. From your personal study of 1 Samuel 2:12-17, explain how Eli's sons consistently sinned against God. Request two volunteers read 1 Samuel 2:22-25 and 3:11-13. Ask: *Do you think Eli set firm limits or just blew off steam when he fussed at his sons? What gives you that impression? What's the difference between scolding and limiting children?* Summarize 1 Samuel 4 to explain how Eli and his sons died. Discuss how the failure of parents to set limits can cause physical, spiritual, or emotional death. Encourage learners to demonstrate love to children by setting and sticking with limits.
5. Lead the class to discuss specific ways adults can display the character qualities listed under "By Leading Them" in Day 2. Allow volunteers to share situations when they intended to scold their children but ended up laughing instead. Explore how parents can achieve the balance between lightening up and setting limits. Discuss how parents can teach their children to laugh even in times of trial. Refer to the Scriptures in the final activity of Day 2 to add to the discussion.
6. Invite a volunteer to read John 10:10. Discuss the first activity in Day 5. Ask what Jesus wants to give. Comment that God's high value of life is reflected in His Sixth Commandment. Ask someone to read that command. Discuss the final activity in Day 3. Guide the class to use the five "c's" displayed on the poster to discuss how adults can help children choose life for themselves and others. Use the principles and activities in Days 3–5 to add to the discussion.
7. Pray for wisdom to teach children to value family and life.

NOTES

Don't Take What's Not Yours

The Key to a Magnificent Marriage

"Thou shalt not commit adultery" (Ex. 20:14).

God wants your marriage to be absolutely splendid, and the key is found in Exodus 20:14. The Seventh Commandment deals with all forms of immorality. What it says in a nutshell is that all sexual involvement outside of marriage, whether premarital or extramarital sex, is a grievous sin against Almighty God.

The Seventh Commandment is repeated and reinforced throughout the New Testament. Jesus told the rich young ruler, "Thou shalt not commit adultery" (Matt. 19:18). First Corinthians 10:8 says, "Neither let us commit fornication." Paul wrote in Colossians 3:5, "Mortify therefore your members which are upon the earth; fornication, uncleanness, inordinate affection, evil concupiscence." And in 1 Thessalonians 4:3 the apostle says, "This is the will of God, even your sanctification, that ye should abstain from fornication."

The Seventh Commandment also speaks to you if you are unmarried but sexually active. You are sinning against God and against the person you will marry. And you're building barriers that you will have to overcome after you get married.

Many of us who have children and grandchildren are wondering who they will marry. Will there be a person who is sexually pure available for them to marry? How are our children going to find the right person? We must teach them to be the right person, because if they are the right person they will have a much greater hope of finding the right person.

Week of JULY 3

Read 1 Thessalonians 4:3-8 in your Bible. Using principles from this passage, list on the chart below the dos and don'ts children must learn to become the right person for a marriage partner.

Do	Don't

THE STATE OF MODERN MARRIAGE

Marriage today is often like a mountain with a beautiful valley at the bottom. There's a winding road coming down the mountainside, full of steep cliffs and sharp precipices. There are obstacles in the road and few, if any, guardrails. At the top of the mountain, a car is starting down the road.

In that car are two newlyweds, heading toward the happy valley of blissful marriage. Along the way they pick up some passengers, but all along that road there are wrecks and other automobiles careening over the precipices or running into the obstacles.

The people in the other cars are being broken and maimed, and the passengers they've picked up are being broken and crushed too. The couples driving those cars thought that when they started toward the happy valley, it was going to be a wonderful and easy trip. But something happened along the way.

That's an illustration of marriage in America today. What should we do? We need to have a heart of love and kindness and let these broken people know that our hearts and churches are open to them. The Word of God has something to say to them. God loves them. God is a God who forgives and restores through Jesus Christ and does not hold grudges.

A second thing we need to do is build some guardrails along the road to the happy valley. We need to remove some of the obstacles that are causing these disastrous marital wrecks. But the main thing we need to do is teach young men and women how to "drive"! Engaged couples or newlyweds could benefit greatly from spending time with a happily married older couple. The church can help young people by faithfully teaching and modeling God's precepts for marriage.

Look up the following Scriptures. From each passage, identify keys for "driving" a safe, happy marriage.
Proverbs 5:15-20 _____
Proverbs 21:17-20 _____
Ecclesiastes 4:9-12 _____
Romans 13:7-8 _____
Ephesians 4:29 _____

What we have is a vicious cycle of broken homes producing broken people who marry other broken people and produce new broken homes. We can break that cycle by showing our young people how to have godly marriages.

God's Plan for Marriage

What is God's plan for marriage? Genesis 2:21-24 gives it to us in just a few verses that contain in principle every problem a marriage will face and the answer to those problems.

THE PRIORITY OF MARRIAGE

The verbs *leave* and *cleave* in Genesis 2:24 tell us that marriage has the highest priority. The highest priority in family life is not parent to child or child to parent but mate to mate. The permanent union of marriage takes precedence over the temporary task of child rearing.

Therefore, parents must prepare their children to leave. But many parents don't want to have an empty nest, so they make it easy for the children to stay. That's a mistake. When we overly pamper our children, we're not equipping them to fly on their own. We're actually handicapping them when it comes to building successful homes themselves.

Parents who pamper their kids often excuse it by saying, "I just want to give my children all the things my parents were never able to give me." The question is not whether you are giving your children the things your parents didn't give you. The question is, are you giving them the things

"The LORD God caused a deep sleep to fall upon Adam, and he slept; and he took one of his ribs, and closed up the flesh instead thereof. And the rib, which the LORD God had taken from man, made he a woman, and brought her unto the man. And Adam said, This is now bone of my bones, and flesh of my flesh: she shall be called Woman, because she was taken out of Man. Therefore shall a man leave his father and his mother, and shall cleave unto his wife: and they shall be one flesh" (Gen. 2:21-24).

Week of JULY 3

your parents did give you? I'm talking about the values and commitments that make for magnificent marriages.

The Bible teaches that a priority must be placed on marriage. After the Lord, your mate is your supreme commitment.

Rank your priorities from 1 (highest) to 6 (lowest).
___ my extended family   ___ God
___ my spouse   ___ my children
___ my occupation   ___ other: _____

THE PERMANENCE OF MARRIAGE

Genesis 2:24 teaches the permanence of marriage as well. The Bible says the man "shall cleave unto his wife." The Hebrew word has the idea of joining or gluing two things together. It's not the partners in a marriage who glue themselves together. God does.

Jesus said in Mark 10:9, "What therefore God hath joined together, let not man put asunder." Marriage is permanent. Marriage is "till death us do part." Show me two young people who consider divorce an option, and I'll show you two young people who have a greatly increased potential for a breakup of their marriage.

People say, "We got divorced because we had problems." People who stay married and people who get divorced have basically the same kinds of problems. The difference is not in the problems. The difference is the commitment to solving them.

THE PURPOSE OF MARRIAGE

"They shall be one flesh." This deals with more than the sexual union of a husband and wife. It means "one flesh" emotionally and spiritually as well.

Marriage is a romance in which both the hero and heroine die in the first chapter. But it's okay because they become one new person. Marriage is much like a violin. A violin without a bow produces no music. A bow without a violin produces no music. But when the two come together, they make beautiful music. God takes two people and makes them one.

Read Hebrews 13:4 in your Bible. Who should honor marriage? _____

State specific ways you will honor your marriage to:

your spouse _____

your children _____

If you are unmarried, what specific things will you do to show you honor the institution of marriage?

_____

God's Warning for Marriage

We need to warn our children about the harm and the heartbreak that come to those who violate God's Seventh Commandment. To *adulterate* means to make impure. When you adulterate the purity of singleness or the sanctity of marriage, you have made impure something that God values very highly.

Read 1 Corinthians 6:18 in your Bible (leave it open to chapter 6, you'll need it again). What makes sexual immorality a particularly destructive sin?

_____

_____

"Righteousness exalteth a nation: but sin is a reproach to any people" (Prov. 14:34).

"If a man be found lying with a woman married to a husband, then they shall both of them die, both the man that lay with the woman, and the woman: so shalt thou put away evil from Israel" (Deut. 22:22).

Adultery is a sin against yourself. There's no sin that will do you more spiritual, psychological, and physical damage than immorality. Everyone is talking today about so-called safe sex. But sex is not supposed to be dangerous. It is supposed to be sacred. Adultery is a sin against your own body.

One of the most heinous things about adultery is what it does to a home and to the children in that home. The lives of innocent children are being torn apart in America by the sin of adultery.

Week of JULY 3

Mothers and fathers who commit adultery are making a devastating statement to their children about how little they value their mate and how little fidelity means to them. They are also teaching their children that honor and commitment are not as important as momentary pleasure.

Read in 1 Corinthians 6:19-20 what adults should teach children. How would you state the truth of this passage to your children at their present stages of development? (If you don't have children, picture yourself talking to a teenager in your church.)

_____

_____

It is Almighty God who said, "Thou shalt not commit adultery." Don't get the idea that a pure life is just an option you may choose as a Christian. If you're not living a life of sexual purity, you have no right to call yourself a Christian. Look at what the Bible says in 1 Corinthians 6:9-10; Ephesians 5:5; and Revelation 21:8 printed in the margin. No matter how you glamorize it, God says immorality is a sin against Him.

God's plan, God's command, is purity, both inside and outside of marriage. If you've failed, God will forgive you if you come to Him with an open and repentant heart. If you have a broken heart or a broken home, bring it to Jesus. He can put it back together if you give Him all the pieces.

After you have repented of impurity in your life, claim God's promise of forgiveness in 1 John 1:9.

When you commit yourself to obey God, He can give you a magnificent marriage. Determine to keep yourself pure before Him, and watch how He will bless you.

Read Psalm 119:9. What must you and your children do to remain true to your commitment to purity?
❏ try really hard
❏ move to a desert island with no TV, radio, magazines, or teenagers
❏ read, study, and obey the Bible

"Know ye not that the unrighteous shall not inherit the kingdom of God? Be not deceived: neither fornicators, nor idolaters, nor adulterers, nor effeminate, nor abusers of themselves with mankind … shall inherit the kingdom of God" (1 Cor. 6:9-10).

"This ye know, that no whoremonger, nor unclean person … hath any inheritance in the kingdom of Christ and of God" (Eph. 5:5).

"The fearful, and unbelieving, and the abominable, and murderers, and whoremongers … shall have their part in the lake which burneth with fire and brimstone: which is the second death" (Rev. 21:8).

day Four

Honesty: Don't Leave Home Without It

"Thou shalt not steal" (Ex. 20:15).

Anytime we take something that belongs to someone else or withhold what rightly belongs to another, we have transgressed this Commandment. Whether it's time, money, affection, possessions, appreciation, love, or anything else, if we defraud somebody else, we are guilty of stealing.

We teach our children what the Eighth Commandment means by teaching them what it means to live with honesty and integrity. Ephesians 4:28 is the perfect explanation and amplification of this Commandment.

Look up Ephesians 4:28 and write it in the margin.

This is a dynamite verse, packed with three principles that need to be emblazoned on the heart of every child.

The first principle is integrity: "Let him that stole steal no more." The second is industry: "Let him labor, working with his hands the thing which is good." And the third is generosity: "That he may have to give to him that needeth."

There are many ways you can live without integrity. Let's talk about the problem and consider some solutions.

DIRECT THEFT

The most obvious violation of the Eighth Commandment is direct stealing through crimes such as shoplifting, armed robbery, and burglary. Our cities are plagued with these things. Shoplifting touches the home more directly because many children and young people are committing this crime as a prank or on a dare.

Stealing at the workplace is epidemic. The American economy loses $40 billion annually from theft on the job. That's everything from pilfering to embezzlement.

Week of JULY 3

FRAUD
Another form of stealing is fraud, or what we call white-collar crime. Halfhearted work is also stealing. If you don't give your employer an honest day's labor, you've stolen from him. If you're an employer and you don't pay your employees what they're worth, you have stolen from them.

Some people breaking the Eighth Commandment think of themselves as shrewd in business. Tax planning is one thing; tax evasion is something else. Having insurance is one thing; insurance fraud is something else. Jesus warned about the scribes who "devour widows' houses" (Mark 12:38-40). They sought opportunities to take advantage of defenseless and unsuspecting widows who did not know how to protect themselves.

GAMBLING
Isn't it sad that one of the greatest forms of thievery in America is perfectly legal in so many places? Gambling is morally wrong. Why? Because nobody can win at gambling without somebody else losing.

Gambling promises happiness but delivers disappointment and frustration. Gambling is profit and pleasure at the cost of somebody else's pain and loss. It's an attempt to get what belongs to someone else without giving him anything for it.

WITHHOLDING LOVE
Withholding love and devotion from those to whom it is due also causes us to break this Commandment. Husbands and wives are not to defraud each other in the matter of sexual love (1 Cor. 7:5). We are also not to withhold neighborly love. "Owe no man any thing, but to love one another" (Rom. 13:8). "Thou shalt love thy neighbor as thyself" (Matt. 22:39).

STEALING FROM YOURSELF
When we steal from others by any of the means we have discussed, we are really stealing from ourselves. "Your iniquities have turned away these things, and your sins have withholden good things from you" (Jer. 5:25). We defraud ourselves when we attempt to defraud others.

STEALING FROM GOD
The worst form of thievery is to steal from God. You ask, "How can we steal from God?" Have you given Him your life? Then You belong to Him.

You are God's by creation. You are His by redemption. He gave Christ to die for you. When you walk God's earth, breathe His air, and live with the life He gave you without pouring that life back out in devotion to Him, the Bible says you are a thief. Everything you have belongs to Him.

Review the headings into today's material and draw a star next to the ways you have broken the Eighth Commandment. How is God calling you to respond?

A Lost Generation

THE IMPORTANCE OF INDUSTRY

If you want a home that is successful in God's eyes, and if you want to help your children have the same, start early in teaching them industry. Even the smallest child can do something to help out and gain that sense of satisfaction and accomplishment that only comes from a job well done.

Sometimes it's easier to do the job yourself than to help your child do it. But getting the job done is not the only goal. Helping him or her learn to work is the goal.

School and after-school activities are part of a child's work—homework, paper routes, baby-sitting, music lessons, sports practices, or whatever else. These are great opportunities for teaching children to stay with a job until it is finished.

Draw a line from each Scripture reference to the truth we must teach children about work.

Proverbs 6:6-11   Work is a gift from God.
Proverbs 10:26   Work is rewarding.
Proverbs 12:14   Laziness is destructive.
Ecclesiastes 3:12-13,22   Lazy people are unpleasant to be around.

Write each of your children's names below. Next to each name write that child's jobs and responsibilities.

_____

_____

_____

_____

Pray about how you can teach biblical truths about work and idleness to your children through their responsibilities. Ask the Lord for wisdom in assigning chores to your children and for courage to cut back on their activities if they are overloaded.

Week of JULY 3

THE JOY OF GENEROSITY

Here's my final point in this matter of obeying the Eighth Commandment and teaching your children to do the same. Just as Ephesians 4:28 teaches integrity and industry, it also teaches generosity: "Let him labor ... that he may have to give to him that needeth."

The opposite of taking from others what you have not earned is giving to others what you have earned. We need to teach our children to work, not only to meet their own needs but to help meet the needs of others.

According to Acts 20:33-35, why did Paul work? (check all that apply)
- ❑ to be as financially secure as everyone else
- ❑ because no one would help him out financially
- ❑ to meet the needs of himself and his companions
- ❑ to be able to give to those in need

> "Misery comes from mirrors; but joy comes from windows when we open our lives and begin to give to others."
> —Adrian Rogers

Working with integrity and industry so we can give to others frees us from a life of selfishness. Children who learn to be selfish are going to be miserable adults. Misery comes from mirrors; but joy comes from windows, when we open our lives and begin to give to others. Train them in giving by precept and by your example.

What truth about giving did Paul learn in Acts 20:35?

_____

In the margin, list specific ways you can teach others this truth by your example.

GIVING OF YOURSELF

Jesus poured out His life's blood for us on the cross. We belong to Him. Don't steal from God by withholding full surrender and service.

When you give yourself to Jesus, He gives something back to you—abundant and eternal life (John 10:10). Whatever you give up for Him cannot compare to the joy of what He gives to you!

Amy SUMMERS

leader Guide

NOTES

To the Leader:

You will notice the majority of today's teaching plan focuses on the Seventh Commandment. The reason for that is simple—one of the greatest concerns of Christian parents today is the sexual purity of their children. Even if child-rearing isn't a major issue for your class—sexuality is. Pray for tact, compassion, and sensitivity as you prepare to guide your class to study what God's Word says about taking only what is yours.

Before the Session:

1. For each participant, glue two pieces of paper together. (You can demonstrate this with just one set of glued papers, but it will be more effective if participants have their own.)

During the Session:

1. In your own words, retell Dr. Roger's marriage parable from Day 1. Ask: *Besides children, what do married couples pick up along the way in their journey? How can these passengers wreck a couple or keep them safely on the road? Who is affected if the car wrecks?* Remark that the Seventh Commandment is a God-given guardrail to prevent the heartache of wrecked homes. OR Distribute to each participant the glued-together papers. Request participants separate the papers. Ask: *What happened to the one paper I gave you?* Comment God glues a man and woman together in marriage; disobedience to the Seventh Commandment rips that whole into tattered shreds.

2. Ask someone to read aloud the Seventh Commandment. Ask how this Commandment speaks to all persons regardless of marital status. Comment that Dr. Rogers said the church must teach young people how to "drive" their marriage. (If you used the second option in number 1, you'll want to briefly summarize the marriage parable from Day 1.) Ask, *How is teaching sexual purity before marriage a lesson in defensive driving?* Discuss keys for marriage, using the second activity in Day 1. Invite participants to state additional keys to a healthy marriage. Challenge learners to think of ways your class can model these keys to younger couples in your church.

3. Comment: *God has a plan for marriage. Only by following His road map can couples make it safely down the mountain.* Invite someone to read Genesis 2:21-24. Briefly explain the priority, permanence, and purpose of marriage. Ask how sexual immorality, before and after marriage, devastates all three aspects of God's plan.

4. Ask: *What does the world teach kids about sex? Whose responsibility is it to teach children God's plan for human sexuality?* Guide the class to

Week of JULY 3

complete the first activity in Day 1. Discuss specific ways to teach children those dos and don'ts. Ask: *How do we deal with the influence of TV, movies, music, and current fashion—do we ban everything or set limits, listen, and look for teachable moments? How do we do either one and still earn our children's honor?* Invite someone to read 1 Corinthians 6:18. Ask participants to state a one-word lesson we need to teach teenagers about tempting sexual situations. [Run!] Direct learners to listen for how Joseph followed principles for sexual purity as you read aloud Genesis 39:6-12. Call for responses. Comment that adults and children need to realize many sexually tempting situations may seem innocent at first and well-mannered people might think it is rude to reject or run from that situation. We must follow Joseph's example and remember the main goal is to be pure, not polite!

5. State that parents can begin laying the groundwork for sexual purity with young children by teaching the principle of 1 Corinthians 6:19-20. Discuss the second activity of Day 3. Explore how adults can teach children this truth when they're doing something negative with their bodies (such as eating junk food, camping out in front of a video game, or wearing immodest clothing) and when they treat their bodies positively (such as healthy eating and physical activity). Discuss how and when this kind of conversation can lead to a discussion of sexual purity.

6. Discuss responses to the first activity of Day 4. Read Ephesians 4:28 and ask learners if they agree this verse is a perfect explanation of the Eighth Commandment and why. Ask if learners believe it is more difficult to instill integrity, industry, or generosity in children. Spend the majority of your remaining time discussing the material and learning activities related to the virtue learners indicated was the most difficult to instill. Discuss specific ways adults can model all three virtues to children.

7. Read aloud 1 Corinthians 2:9 and the last sentence of Day 5. Declare that it is the Christian adult's task to encourage children that whatever they give up in terms of popularity, instant gratification, time, or money is worth the joy of an abundant life in Christ. Pray for the adults in your class to have the wisdom and courage to be equal to that task.

NOTES

Adrian ROGERS

Truth and Satisfaction

The Liability of a False Witness

"Thou shalt not bear false witness against thy neighbor" (Ex. 20:16).

I mentioned earlier that America has lost its sense of basic honesty. It seems that we as a people have set aside and disregarded the Ninth Commandment. I want to help you teach your children to love honesty, to speak and live the truth. But we need to do a little blasting before we can build. So let's talk about the loss of absolute truth, then see from God's Word what we can do about it.

Read John 8:44 in your Bible. Who is the father, the source, of all false witness? _____

1. ___ "At the same time, they also learn to be idle, going from house to house; they are not only idle, but are also gossips and busybodies, saying things they shouldn't say" (1 Tim. 5:13, HCSB).

Every time you tell a lie, you're acting like the Devil. You need to understand and communicate this vital truth to your children. Lies aren't funny or clever; they aren't "black" or "white." They are sin, every one of them. Let's look at some of the sins of the tongue for which God holds us liable.

After you read about each sin of the tongue below, write the letter of each topic (A,B,C,D,E,F) next to the Scripture in the margin that speaks against that sin.

2. ___ "You must not go about spreading slander among your people; you must not jeopardize your neighbor's life; I am the Lord" (Lev. 19:16, HCSB).

A. SLANDER

When you slander, you're like the Devil. But when you tell the truth, you're like the Lord Jesus, who is "the truth" (John 14:6).

In the garden of Eden Satan used slander to corrupt our first parents. Satan slandered God's character and God's honesty. Satan also used slander and false witness to criticize Job (see Job 1:10). To attack God's

Week of JULY 10

people is one thing, but Satan was not content with that. He even came against the Lord Jesus Christ Himself with his lies and temptations in the wilderness (see Matt. 4:1-11).

Satan is still bearing false witness against Jesus today. Anytime you hear someone deny the Lord's deity and the truth of His Word, you are hearing a false witness the Devil has scoured up.

B. PERJURY

Satan is in the business of lying. It doesn't matter what people think. Your calling from God is to speak the truth. If you perjure yourself in a courtroom, one day you will answer for that in God's courtroom. The one who accuses the innocent will suffer the penalty the innocent person suffered.

C. SPREADING RUMORS

Rumors spread so much faster than the truth. Have you ever wondered why rumors are so popular, so readily listened to and spread by so many people? It's another evidence that the slanderer is still at work.

If you are one who is given to receiving and spreading rumors, you need to know that you are courting the discipline of Almighty God.

D. FLATTERY

Did you know that flattery is forbidden in the Word of God? I'm not talking about giving encouragement. You ought to give encouragement. I'm not talking about giving thanks. You ought to give thanks. I'm not talking about giving honor where honor is due. Encouragement, thanksgiving, and honor are oil that lubricate life.

A flatterer will say to your face what he will not say behind your back. A hypocrite will say behind your back what he will not say to your face. They are heads and tails of the same evil coin. God's Word forbids both.

E. INSINUATION

On one occasion when Jesus Christ was teaching, the Pharisees insinuated that He was an illegitimate child. The implication was Jesus was a product of fornication. What a horrible insinuation! It was a lie.

You can bear false witness by insinuation, by the tone of your voice, even by the arching of your eyebrows. You can also bear false witness by what you don't say.

3. ___ "A wicked person listens to malicious talk; a liar pays attention to a destructive tongue" (Prov. 17:4, HCSB).

4. ___ "You must not spread a false report. Do not join the wicked to be a malicious witness. You must not follow a crowd in wrongdoing. Do not testify in a lawsuit and go along with a crowd to pervert justice" (Ex. 23:1-2, HCSB).

5. ___ "A lying mouth hates those it crushes, and a flattering mouth causes ruin" (Prov. 26:28, HCSB).

6. ___ "A worthless person, a wicked man, who goes around speaking dishonestly, who winks his eyes, signals with his feet, and gestures with his fingers" (Prov. 6:12-13, HCSB).

F. Listening to the Lie

When you listen to a falsehood, you're as liable as the false witness who gives it. In some cases, you can even break the spirit of the Ninth Commandment by simply being silent, by not speaking up to affirm truth or to stop a lie.

> **Read Psalm 5:9; Proverbs 15:4; and 16:28 in your Bible. Complete the statements as if you were teaching a child what God's Word says about lying:**
>
> **When you lie** _____
>
> **When you are truthful** _____

day Two

The Reliability of a Faithful Witness

Now that we know how God views those who bear false witness, I want to introduce you to a faithful witness and show you what it means to be a person who not only believes the truth but lives it.

Micaiah – mi cay' uh

The faithful witness I want you to meet is the Old Testament prophet Micaiah (see 1 Kings 22). He lived in the days of wicked King Ahab of Israel and Jehoshaphat, the good king of Judah.

Jehoshaphat was a good king, but he got in serious trouble because he couldn't face the truth. As the story progressed, he failed to rely on the only faithful witness in Ahab's entire court, the prophet Micaiah.

Ahab and Jehoshaphat made their battle plans and then decided to consult the Lord. That's backward, so they were in trouble already. When Jehoshaphat asked Ahab to seek a word from the Lord, Ahab called together his 400 pandering, pussy-footing prophets, who rubber-stamped the decision he had already made. "Go up," they all said, "for the LORD shall deliver it into the hand of the king" (vv. 5-6).

Jehoshaphat must have been a little skeptical about 400 preachers agreeing so completely on something. He asked Ahab, "Is there not here a

Week of JULY 10

prophet of the LORD besides, that we might inquire of him?" (v. 7). Ahab said there was one more, Micaiah.

According to 1 Kings 22:8, how did Ahab feel about Micaiah? _____
Why? (check your answer)
❏ They were of different political parties.
❏ Micaiah didn't bathe very often.
❏ Micaiah told Ahab the truth.
❏ Micaiah wasn't nice to Ahab.

Nevertheless, they sent for Micaiah. The messenger who came to get him warned him that all of Ahab's prophets had already prophesied success, so Micaiah better just add his own word of blessing (v. 13).

"Micaiah said, 'As the LORD liveth, what the LORD saith unto me, that will I speak'" (v. 14). Micaiah's reward for telling the truth was a punch in the face and a stint in prison. But all things happened just as Micaiah had prophesied.

This is such a powerful example of what it takes to be a faithful witness that I want to share with you five principles that will help you and your children be truthful witnesses as the Ninth Commandment requires.

1. It is better to be divided by truth than united in error. This is the first thing we learn from Micaiah's life. We are to keep the unity of the Spirit (Eph. 4:3), but don't sacrifice the truth on the altar of unity. Unity in the truth? Yes. But unification and uniformity where truth is sacrificed? Never.

2. It is better to tell the truth that hurts and then heals than to tell a lie that comforts and then kills. Four hundred prophets told King Ahab a lie that comforted him in the short run but eventually killed him. One prophet, Micaiah, refused to give Ahab false comfort. Ahab hated the message that would have saved his life, and he hated the messenger who delivered it. Rough truth is better than polished falsehood.

Read Proverbs 27:5-6 in the margin. Do you more often seek out and appreciate the ❏ **honest wounds of a friend? OR** ❏ **deceitful kisses of an enemy? Do you more often give:** ❏ **honest wounds? OR** ❏ **deceitful kisses?**

"Open rebuke is better than secret love. Faithful are the wounds of a friend; but the kisses of an enemy are deceitful" (Prov. 27:5-6, KJV).

69

3. It is better to be hated for telling the truth than to be loved for telling a lie. Ahab said of Micaiah, "I hate him." You need to help your children understand that if they tell the truth, they may not get elected "most popular" at school. But if they tell the truth and suffer for it, they are in good company.

> **Read the following Scriptures in your Bible and complete each statement.**
> **1 Kings 22:26-27: Micaiah told the truth and he was**
> _____
> **John 8:40: Jesus told the truth and He was**
> _____
> **Think about your own life: I told the truth and I was**
> _____

4. It is better to stand alone with the truth than to be wrong with a multitude. The majority is frequently wrong. Think of Noah. He and his family stood alone and went into the ark a minority. But they came out a majority!

You may be called on to stand alone for truth just as Micaiah was. Your children may have to stand alone for truth in their classrooms. We need to arm ourselves with the truth and prepare our children to stand for it.

5. It is better to ultimately succeed with the truth than to temporarily succeed with a lie. Ahab went into battle, and God's arrow found him. But God's crown found Micaiah. The Word of God is the only thing that will stand the test of time and ultimately succeed.

The Responsibility of a Family Witness

How do we take these things we have talked about and teach them to our children, so they might permeate society with truth? Let me give you three basic ways.

Week of JULY 10

TEACH BY PRECEPT

Get out God's Word and show your children what it says about telling the truth. Teach them God's precepts. Show your kids that when they tell a lie, they're acting like the Devil. And when they tell the truth, they're acting like the Lord Jesus Christ.

Don't just say, "Don't lie." Give them biblical reasons. Tell your children why they ought to tell the truth. Make certain your children understand God's holy Commandments.

Read Psalm 15:1-3 and 34:11-13 in your Bible and complete the chart. (Even better, ask your child to help you fill in the chart.)

What God commands	Why God commands this

TEACH BY EXAMPLE

Be a godly example. Both fathers and mothers need to be able to say to their children, "God says we are not to lie. As He is my witness and my helper, I will never lie to you. I will always keep my word to you." You can fail in many ways and still come out on the plus side with your children. But if you fail to keep your word, if you fail to tell your children the truth, your home is on the road to disaster.

Admit it when you've done wrong. Let your children know that you are a truth-speaker. Teach your children by example. Live the Word of God in your home. Tell the truth to your children, and keep your word.

Read Proverbs 11:13 in your Bible. List ways a parent might betray a child's confidence.

If you have been untruthful to your children (or loved one) in any way, ask their forgiveness and openly commit to truth in your relationship.

Teach by Discipline

There were three deadly D's our kids knew about when they were growing up, three things they knew their parents would not put up with.

The first is deliberate disobedience. A child can disobey in a way that is not arrogant or deliberate. In those cases, deal gently with the child. But deliberate disobedience must be dealt with immediately and decisively.

The second is defiance. That's disobedience with a disrespectful attitude—a defiant disrespect for authority.

The third is dishonesty. God's judgment is sure on those who bear false witness. We can spare our children God's discipline by dealing immediately, kindly, and yet sternly with dishonesty.

Using Psalm 141:3 and Proverbs 30:7-8 (in the margin) as a guide, pray for honesty to flourish in your home.

"LORD, set up a guard for my mouth; keep watch at the door of my lips" (Ps. 141:3, HCSB).

"Two things I ask of You; don't deny them to me before I die: Keep falsehood and deceitful words far from me. Give me neither poverty nor wealth; feed me with the food I need" (Prov. 30:7-8, HCSB).

day four

The Secret of Satisfaction

We have been told that we cannot be happy unless we have something that's newer, bigger, better, and shinier than what we already have. But the truth is, this desire for more and more is making us unhappy.

Name an item you've seen advertised lately. _____

What does it promise? _____

How might that advertised item make you unhappy or dissatisfied? _____

"Thou shalt not covet thy neighbor's house, thou shalt not covet thy neighbor's wife, nor his manservant, nor his maidservant, nor his ox, nor his ass, nor any thing that is thy neighbor's" (Ex. 20:17).

The Tenth Commandment says not to covet. *To covet* means to have an unlawful desire for that which is not rightfully yours. Covetousness is not limited to money. It could involve influence, fame, power, or appearance.

The Tenth Commandment is not a command against lawful desire. When God saves you, He doesn't neuter you. He doesn't make you a person without passion. It's not wrong to have godly ambition.

Week of JULY 10

It's not necessarily wrong to desire things. God knows you want to love and be loved. You have a God-given desire for friendship and a home, for happiness, joy, success, victory, peace. These things are not wrong. They are from God.

Read 1 Timothy 6:17 in your Bible. In the statement below, mark out each incorrect term and write above it a word that will transform it into a true statement.

God meagerly provides some things for us to get by.

A Perplexing Problem

The first thing I want you to notice as we consider the secret of satisfaction is the perplexing problem of covetousness. Do you know why it's such a big problem?

Covetousness is terribly deceitful. Very few people even realize they are covetous because we become so used to it.

Is covetousness a sin of   action? OR attitude? (circle) Briefly describe how breaking the Tenth Commandment can lead to breaking any of the other nine.

_____

"Every good gift and every perfect gift is from above, and cometh down from the Father of lights, with whom is no variableness, neither shadow of turning" (Jas. 1:17).

Until we get to the root of the problem we'll never get to a solution.

Covetousness is an octopus that wraps itself around your soul. And the trouble with a covetous person is that he not only poisons his own life with misery, but he spoils everyone and everything else he touches.

When you have covetousness in your heart, when you have this unlawful desire, your life is bent and broken and you destroy others. As I said above, covetousness is an octopus that will wrap itself around your soul and literally drag you into hell.

Does that sound too harsh? Read what the Apostle Paul said in Ephesians 5:5: "This ye know, that no whoremonger, nor unclean person, nor covetous man, who is an idolater, hath any inheritance in the kingdom of Christ and of God." God links covetousness with whoremongering, perversion, and idolatry. Don't think this is a small sin. It is the root of all the rest.

day Five

A Proper Perspective

Since covetousness is such a perplexing problem, how do we deal with it? We've got to back off and get a proper perspective on the whole thing. We need to understand who we are and what we have, especially as we think about how to teach our children the truth of the Tenth Commandment.

Hebrews 13:5 is a good place to start. Here is the secret of satisfaction and the answer to covetousness: "Let your conversation [your lifestyle] be without covetousness; and be content with such things as ye have: for he [God] hath said, I will never leave thee, nor forsake thee."

You will always be covetous until you learn contentment. Why? Because all of us need satisfaction, and covetousness in essence means trying to find satisfaction in the wrong place. The secret of satisfaction is to be content with what you have.

"Godliness with contentment is great gain" (1 Tim. 6:6, KJV).

"I have learned to be content in whatever circumstances I am. I know both how to have a little, and I know how to have a lot. In any and all circumstances I have learned the secret of being content ... I am able to do all things through Him who strengthens me" (Phil. 4:11-13, HCSB).

Read the Scriptures in the margin. Circle the value of contentment and underline the secret to contentment.

WHAT YOU HAVE

If you're a child of God, you have abundance. You have God Himself. You have Him, and He has you.

You have your family. "Whoso findeth a wife findeth a good thing" (Prov. 18:22). "Lo, children are a heritage of the LORD" (Ps. 127:3). If you have children, count your blessings. Thank God for them. They are a heritage from the Lord.

You have friends. "A friend loveth at all times" (Prov. 17:17). It's wonderful to be loved and to know it! If you have friends, you are a wealthy person.

You have God's wisdom. If you have discovered godly wisdom, how rich you are. "Happy is the man that findeth wisdom, and the man that getteth understanding: for the merchandise of it is better than the merchandise of silver, and the gain thereof than fine gold" (Prov. 3:13-14).

Week of JULY 10

Can you say like Paul that you have learned to be content in all circumstances?
    ❑ Yes   ❑ No   ❑ Sometimes
Can you say not only that Jesus is necessary but that He's enough?   ❑ Yes   ❑ No   ❑ Sometimes

If you can say that Jesus is enough, you have satisfaction.

WHAT YOU NEED

If you have Jesus, you have the peace of God that passes all understanding. You are a rich person. But if you don't have Jesus, you need Him more than you have ever needed anything in your life.

What you need is a proper perspective on this matter of covetousness. Understand who you are. Let your life be free of it. God has said He will never leave or forsake you. What more do you need?

THE REAL PROBLEM

Our real problem is not that we break the Ten Commandments. That's only a symptom. The real problem is our hearts. We need to be saved. We need to be born again, because keeping the Ten Commandments won't get anybody to heaven. We have to be saved by receiving Jesus Christ as our Lord and Savior. Then He will give us the power to live as we ought to live.

If you have never trusted Jesus as your Savior, or if you're not sure of your standing before Him, I invite you to pray this simple prayer right now:

Jesus, You died to save me, and You promised to save me if I would trust You. I do trust You, Lord Jesus. I believe You're the Son of God. I believe You paid my sin-debt with Your blood on the cross. I believe that God raised You from the dead. And now by faith I receive You into my life as my Lord and Savior. I'm sorry for my sin. I turn from my sin. Forgive me. Cleanse me. Come into my life, and begin now to make me the person You want me to be. Amen.

If you know Jesus, then you know that the secret of satisfaction isn't found in anything on earth. It's found only in Him!

If you just asked Christ into your life, notify your Bible study leader or pastor of your decision.

If you are already a believer, write Psalm 90:14 in the margin, in the form of a prayer.

For further help on accepting Christ as your Savior, turn to the "How To Become a Christian" article on the inside of the front cover.

NOTES

To the Leader:

Do you want to ask questions that generate interest and discussion among class participants? Listen to what they talk about before and after class and gear questions to those issues.

Before the Session:

1. Make certain the Ten Commandments poster you made for Week 1 and the 5 "c's" poster you made in Week 2 are still displayed.
2. Secure a dictionary definition of *slander*.

During the Session:

1. Ask the class for terms people use for the word *lie*. (Samples: *half-truth, little white lie, fib, story, stretch the truth*) Ask why people use those terms. Inquire: *According to the popular worldview, when is dishonesty the best policy? According to the biblical worldview, when is honesty the best policy? Why?* OR Invite volunteers to share policies they are (or were) required to follow at work. (Encourage learners who don't work outside the home to share policies they observe in the community or at school.) Ask, *Of all the policies you have to follow, which would you say is the best policy?* For both options comment that in God's eyes honesty isn't just the best policy, it's a command. Request someone read the Ninth Commandment.

2. To examine the origin of all truth and lies, request someone read John 8:44 and answer the first question in Day 1. Ask: *Do you think it was a coincidence Jesus mentioned murder in the same breath as lying? Why?* Direct learners to read Genesis 3:1-4 in their Bibles and identify the first lie in history. Read the dictionary definition of *slander*. Ask how Satan slandered God. Inquire: *Is all lying slander against God's character? Why?* Read aloud Numbers 23:19 and comment that since God is the Father of all truth, any untruth dishonors His character. Ask the class to identify the Scripture in the margin of Day 1 that speaks against slander (Lev. 19:16). Discuss how slander endangers a person's life. Direct the class to read Genesis 3:8-13 and identify what the first lie by Satan led to (further dishonesty). Guide the class to identify the margin Scriptures that speak against the forms of lying discussed in Day 1. (Suggested answers: 1. C; 2. A; 3. F; 4. B; 5. D; 6. E) Lead a discussion with questions such as: *Why do rumors spread so quickly? How do we put a stop to rumors? How is flattery dishonest?*

Week of JULY 10

Read John 8:41. Ask: *What did the Pharisees insinuate about Jesus? Why is insinuation such a destructive form of dishonesty? How can we refuse to listen to a lie? How might we suffer for refusing to be dishonest in any of these ways?*

3. The story of Micaiah is a perfect example of a person who stood for truth regardless of the circumstances. Summarize 1 Kings 22:1-40. Guide the class to discuss the principles Dr. Rogers drew from this biblical account in Day 2. Ask, *How can we use Micaiah's example and illustrations from our own lives to teach children honesty is worth whatever price we pay to be truthful?* Use the material and learning activities from Day 3 to add to the discussion.

4. Invite someone to read Proverbs 30:7-8 from the margin on page 72. Ask how this prayer for honesty is also a request for help to honor the Tenth Commandment. Ask someone to read the Tenth Commandment. Ask what *covet* means and what people covet. Inquire: *Is it wrong to want things? Support your answer with Scripture. What's the problem with covetousness?* Discuss the last activity of Day 4. Request the class listen for how Paul pointed out that truth to Timothy as a volunteer reads aloud 1 Timothy 6:6-10. Call for responses. Ask them to follow along in their Bibles as you read aloud 1 Timothy 6:11,17-21 and note how Paul's fatherly instructions to Timothy are similar to the principles for teaching the Ten Commandments your class has discussed in the past weeks. Call for responses. (For example: flee; be generous, refuse godless chatter and falsehoods, worship only God)

5. Ask, *What is the remedy for covetousness?* (contentment) Ask the class to state situations where children might be tempted to covet. (toddler wants another child's toy, teen wants a car someone else owns, adolescent isn't happy without expensive brand-name clothing) Request someone read the Scriptures in the margin on page 74. Discuss how parents and those who work with youth and children can use the five "c's" (from Week 1) to teach the principles of contentment in those passages.

6. Remark that children learn contentment best when they see it modeled in their parents. Close in prayer by reading aloud Psalm 90:14.

NOTES

Adrian ROGERS

A Word of Encouragement

day One

Let the Training Begin

"Train up a child in the way he should go: and when he is old, he will not depart from it" (Prov. 22:6).

We have talked about many truths in the preceding weeks. I have tried not only to help you understand and apply the truth of God to your own life, but to teach His commands and precepts to your children.

But the thought of trying to teach God's Word to their children can overwhelm some parents. They look at the whole scope of a project like teaching the Ten Commandments rather than taking things one step at a time, and it seems like too much to get across.

Other parents have tried family devotions or Bible times in various forms and have gotten discouraged for different reasons. So they tend to give up and say, "I just can't make it work."

Still other parents find it hard to get started teaching the Bible in their home because they are bound by guilt. It may be guilt over their own failures or guilt over mistakes they have made with their children. Whatever the cause, these parents feel unworthy to teach the Word to others.

How is the Bible taught in your home?
_____

If you couldn't answer that question, check the reasons why you're not teaching the Bible.
❑ It's too overwhelming, and I don't know enough.
❑ I've tried and it just doesn't work for us.
❑ I'm not worthy to teach it to others.
❑ We're just too busy.
❑ Other: _____

Week of JULY 17

If you fall into any of these categories—or even if you're sailing right along and having regular and wonderful family devotions—I want to offer you a strong word of biblical encouragement. I want you to know and believe that God will help you teach your children, and that He will bless your efforts if you will look to Him and lean on Him.

Consider with me one of the most powerful principles in Scripture—a principle that will, if you heed it in your home, do more than just about anything else to prepare your children to be godly men and women, wise fathers and mothers, and fruitful members of the body of Christ.

My purpose is not to overwhelm you with more information or to heap guilt upon you. By God's grace, I want to encourage, uplift, and equip you for the all-important task of raising your children to know, love, and follow Jesus Christ.

The principle is stated in this very familiar, though often misunderstood, verse: "Train up a child in the way he should go: and when he is old, he will not depart from it" (Prov. 22:6). What wisdom the Bible packs into a few words!

How might Proverbs 22:6 be misunderstood?

How can Proverbs 22:6 give hope to parents?

Tomorrow we'll see what this means by considering four very valuable techniques this verse gives us for training our children.

Commence in Childhood

Notice that Proverbs 22:6 says, "Train up a *child*" (my emphasis). Training is most effective when it begins in the earliest years of childhood.

There are several factors that make early training the most desirable.

THE CORRECTION FACTOR

It is much easier to correct children when they're young and more pliable. You can correct a child, but once he gets to be a man, it's going to be very hard to change him. Proverbs 19:18 has a wise word for us parents: "Chasten thy son while there is hope." We need to teach our children God's Commandments while they are young, open, and teachable.

Proverbs 13:24 says, "He that spareth his rod hateth his son: but he that loveth him chasteneth him betimes." You may say, "My children don't need correcting. They're little angels." I know they're all little angels. But as their legs get longer, you're going to find their wings get shorter! Your children are not little angels dropped down from heaven with halos around their heads. And neither are mine.

Read Psalm 71:5-6,17-18 in your Bible.
When did the psalmist begin to learn about God?
_____

What did he gain from this early training in godliness?
_____

How long did he intend to follow God's way?
_____

THE COMMUNICATION FACTOR

Here is a second factor that argues for early training. Childhood is a wonderful time for communication. Little children have a great ability to learn. One reason for that is their great curiosity. They always want to know why. I know a child's questions get a little wearisome at times, but don't quench that wonderful curiosity. God has built it into your child.

Read Exodus 12:26-27 in your Bible. Hebrew children learned about _____ by asking questions.
Think of a family holiday tradition. _____
When your children ask, "What does this ritual mean to you?" how will you answer? _____
_____
_____
_____

Week of JULY 17

Children also have a great memory capacity. It's amazing what little ones can learn and retain. God has given children a great capacity for learning and memorizing. Besides that, they are humble enough to be taught, and they trust what their parents tell them.

Childhood is the optimum time to communicate God's truth to your children. Tomorrow that toddler won't be asking why. Tomorrow that schoolboy won't be asking for help with his homework. And tomorrow that teenager will not want to hang around the house.

THE CONVERSION FACTOR

Early childhood is also the best time for conversion. We ought to see to it that our children find Christ at an early age. We shouldn't manipulate children—or anyone else, for that matter—into trusting Christ. Children don't need to be tricked or coerced into coming to Jesus. They only need to be guided. It ought to be perfectly normal and natural for children to come to know Jesus as their Savior and Lord if they're raised in a Christian home.

I love Mark 10:13-16, where some parents brought their young children to Jesus so He could touch them. Read those verses in the margin.

The disciples thought Jesus was too busy to be bothered with little children. But He set them straight in a hurry.

> "His disciples rebuked those that brought them. But when Jesus saw it, he was much displeased, and said unto them, 'Suffer the little children to come unto me, and forbid them not: for of such is the kingdom of God. Verily I say unto you, Whosoever shall not receive the kingdom of God as a little child, he shall not enter therein.' And he took them up in his arms, put his hands upon them, and blessed them" (Mark 10:13-16).

Read Matthew 18:1-3 in your Bible. Mark the statements (T) true or (F) false.
___ A little child has to become like an adult to understand the things of God.
___ An adult has to become like a little child to enter God's kingdom.

Children can be and should be saved at an early age. Matthew Henry was saved at the age of 11. Jonathan Edwards was saved at 8. Charles Haddon Spurgeon was saved when he was 12. He later said he would have been saved earlier if there had been someone to instruct and guide him.

In our Southern Baptist Convention, one survey showed that 90 percent of all our missionaries were converted before they were 11. The average age of their conversion was 8.

The early church father Polycarp was converted at 9 years of age and died in the flames for Jesus at 90. Sounds to me like that was a childhood conversion that took! Make it your joy to lead your children to Christ.

Correct with Consistency

A second child-training technique found in Proverbs 22:6 is this: You are to correct with consistency. Let me give you some reasons for that.

BECAUSE GOD SAYS SO

> **Read Proverbs 3:12 and 13:24 in your Bible and complete the equation. Discipline = L _____**

According to God's Word, a father doesn't love his child when he refuses to correct him. No parent is smarter than God. If you love your child, you're going to correct your child.

BECAUSE OF HUMAN NATURE

"Foolishness is bound in the heart of a child; but the rod of correction shall drive it far from him" (Prov. 22:15). The word *foolishness* here means wickedness, in the same sense the term *fool* is used throughout Proverbs. The fool in Proverbs is someone who hates and ignores God and plunges recklessly into sin, to his own destruction. Children need to learn there is a moral authority in this world against which they are not allowed to rebel.

TO SPARE YOURSELF

> **Read Proverbs 29:15,17 in the margin. Circle the negative side of not disciplining children. Underline the positive side of administering discipline.**

"The rod and reproof give wisdom: but a child left to himself bringeth his mother to shame. ... Correct thy son, and he shall give thee rest; yea, he shall give delight unto thy soul" (Prov. 29:15,17).

If you don't discipline your children, one of these days you're going to be ashamed for your lack of consistency. But what a joy to see children who have been well corrected. Stop trying to win a popularity contest with your children; begin planning for their future.

Week of JULY 17

A SPIRITUAL BENEFIT

At first glance Proverbs 23:13-14 (in the margin) sounds awfully cruel. The word *rod* does not mean a club. The writer is talking about a spanking utensil, something that will cause a sting without doing any harm.

The Bible is wise to tell parents to use a spanking utensil rather than their bare hands. Use a neutral instrument for spanking so that your hands can be thought of as instruments of love and caressing.

Spanking needs to be used at the right time, at the right place, in the right way. You can chasten a child without hurting him. And the Bible says that if you will be consistent in this, you'll save your child's soul from hell.

How is that? A child who does not learn to respect authority at home is not going to respect authority in the school, the church, or the government—and will not respect God either.

"Withhold not correction from the child: for if thou beatest him with the rod, he shall not die. Thou shalt beat him with the rod, and shalt deliver his soul from hell" (Prov. 23:13-14).

Read Proverbs 23:15-18. Complete the equation.
Discipline = H _____ and a F _____.

SEVEN RULES FOR DISCIPLINE

1. Begin your discipline early. You should begin to correct a child when that child is old enough to knowingly and willingly disobey.

2. Think of spanking as your last resort, not the first technique you use. Resort to a spanking only when reasoning and warning and instructing have failed to bring about the desired behavior.

We can do more with telling and leading and teaching and explaining than we can with a paddle; so speaking ought to come before spanking.

3. Administer discipline promptly. Especially when it's time for corporal punishment, deliver the discipline as close to the time of the disobedience as possible. Don't let a threat linger over a child's head all day.

4. Parents present a united front in discipline. Don't let one do all the spanking and the other all the hugging. Children are very clever. They will play one parent against another if you let them. Don't fall into that trap.

5. If you decide to spank your child, do a good job. Have you ever seen a mother in a supermarket just kind of swatting at her child? The kid is dodging and feinting like a boxer as the mother flails the air. She's getting madder by the minute, and the child isn't learning anything except when to duck. If you're going to administer a spanking, do it in the right place, at the right time, and in the right way.

The great thing about a good spanking is that you don't have to do it very often. A few good spankings and your spanking days should be more or less over. You shouldn't have to constantly be swatting at your kids.

6. Always discipline in love. Your discipline should always be an expression of your love. The whole point of the Ten Commandments was to cause God's people to love Him with all of their being. When you discipline a child in love, the message is going to come through that this disobedience has broken your heart because you love that child so much.

Read 2 Corinthians 7:9 in your Bible. What should be the goal in godly, parental discipline?

_____

7. Always discipline with a view to repentance. Correction is not a matter of getting even with your child. Nor is the goal simply to administer outward correction. You want to correct the child inwardly also.

When children are old enough to understand the concept of sin, they need to know it not only breaks God's law, but it also breaks His heart.

While repentance may be your desire and your goal, you may not reach it in every case with every child. You cannot be the Holy Spirit in your child's life. You cannot make a child repent, but you can pray that he will. And you can discipline in a way that points the child in the direction of repentance toward God.

If you will do this, God will honor it and use it in your children's lives.

day four

Communicate with Creativity

Proverbs 22:6 contains a very interesting phrase that I believe tells us we should be training our children creatively. "Train up a child *in the way he should go*" (emphasis mine).

Week of JULY 17

A CHILD'S UNIQUENESS

The idea behind this phrase is that every child is an individual. Children are not all the same. Your child carries within him or her a God-given blend of innate talents, interests, personality traits, and yet-to-be-developed spiritual gifts that make him or her unique—one-of-a-kind.

That means you need to be creative in your approach to each of your children. You need God's wisdom to communicate His truth with creativity. God has put a unique bent in that child's personality.

Read Psalm 103:13-14 in the margin. What do you need to remember about your children as you seek to discipline them? _____
_____

"As a father has compassion on his children, so the LORD has compassion on those who fear Him. For He knows what we are made of, remembering that we are dust" (Ps. 103:13-14, HCSB).

TEACHING CREATIVELY

We are often told that we can't teach Bible doctrine to little children, that they're too young to understand it. But even a little one can learn "Jesus loves me, this I know." Those little children can learn to love and reverence God. And they will live what they learn.

That's why a child who is constantly being criticized learns to condemn others. A child who lives with anger and violence learns to fight. A child who is made fun of withdraws into a shell.

But a child who is given encouragement gains the confidence to face life. A child who is treated with fairness develops a sense of justice. A child who is made to feel secure at home learns to trust God. A child who knows he is loved and accepted as he is accepts other people the same way. And a child who receives love gives love.

On this matter of teaching and training with creativity, let me give you a fascinating picture of what this meant in Hebrew culture. In addition to its connotations of dedication and discipline, the word *train* has in its very root the idea of touching something to the palate.

Hebrew mothers didn't have ready-made baby food; so the mother would strain the baby's food by chewing it up herself and then take a little bit of that food and touch it to the part of the baby's palate called the uvula. When the uvula is stimulated it triggers the swallowing impulse. So the mother would put the food in the baby's mouth, and the baby would swallow. That's how Hebrew mothers fed their children.

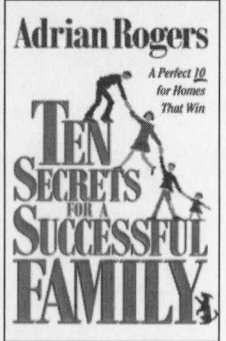

If you have enjoyed these studies from Adrian Rogers and desire to purchase your own copy of his book Ten Secrets for a Successful Family *(ISBN: 1-58134-033-8) to read and study in greater detail, visit the LifeWay Christian Store serving you. Or you can order a copy by calling 1-800-233-1123.*

Look for articles that support **MasterWork** *in Biblical Illustrator Plus beginning in Fall 2005. Place your order for BI Plus, an interactive CD-ROM, on the Dated Literature Order Form or see your minister of education or Sunday School director.*

What a great picture of making the Word of God palatable to our children. We can't just ram it down their throats or they'll choke on it. We must be gentle and kind. That's the problem with so many parents who try to teach the Bible to their kids. They're not teaching it creatively. The idea is, "You sit still while I instill."

What verse or concept from God's Word have you been "chewing" on? _____

How can you "feed" that truth to your children or to a friend? _____

Your children are unique individuals. Find their bent, and guide them in the way God has aimed them. Then you'll find success.

Continue with Confidence

What a wonderful picture Proverbs 22:6 gives us of the proper way to teach and train our children. If you will commence with childhood, correct with consistency, and communicate with creativity, you will continue with confidence because God's Word says, "When [your child] is old, he will not depart from it."

That doesn't mean when your child is a middle-aged adult or an old man. The word *old* here has the idea of hair on the chin. In other words, this is referring to a child who is able to grow a beard, which could even mean a teenager.

I must say a word about this because many brokenhearted Christian parents are clinging to Proverbs 22:6 as they wait for wayward adult children to return to the fold. The proverbs of Scripture are not ironclad promises. They are principles that when applied faithfully will generally

Week of JULY 17

end in a desired result. There is no guarantee because children sometimes make bad decisions of their own.

Alongside the proverb is another factor—human will. Some parents are taking undue blame for the failures of their children, and other parents may be taking undue praise for the sheer grace of God that has given them wonderful kids.

Many parents have the idea that you teach your children about God when they are little, then when they're teenagers they will have a time of rebellion where they leave the right path, but as they grow up they will eventually come back.

I've heard people say, "Well, my son is not living for God, but you know what the Bible says: 'When he is old, he'll not depart from it.'" Proverbs 22:6 doesn't promise he will come back. I know of no Bible promise that says a wayward child is certain to come back to Christ.

In the mercy of God he may return to the faith. Many older children have. But that's not what Proverbs 22:6 is talking about. It's a tremendous word of encouragement and exhortation to raise your children in the nurture and admonition of the Lord.

You say, "But my children aren't little anymore." Then start where you are. And if they're already grown, pray for them. God is so merciful!

You can have a successful home if you'll teach God's Ten Commandments to your children. You can bring your children to Christ, and you can bring them up for Christ.

It means more to me than anything to know that my children love the Lord Jesus Christ. When I take my children and grandchildren home to heaven with me, I'll say, "Thank You, Lord Jesus, it was worth it all."

Will you be able to say that? I trust you will. May God bless you and help you make your home a little touch of heaven on earth!

Write a prayer below for your children, using Proverbs 23:22-25 in the margin as a guide.

_____

_____

_____

_____

Four Techniques for Training Our Children:

1. Commence with childhood
2. Correct with consistency
3. Communicate with creativity
4. Continue with confidence
   —Adrian Rogers

"Listen to your father who gave you life, and don't despise your mother when she is old. Buy—and do not sell—truth, wisdom, instruction, and understanding. The father of a righteous son will rejoice greatly, and one who fathers a wise son will delight in him. Let your father and mother have joy, and let her who gave birth to you rejoice" (Prov. 23:22-25, HCSB).

NOTES

To the Leader:

Read Psalm 78:1-7. As a teacher of adults, how are you involved in teaching God's Word to the children in your church? One of the greatest ways you can influence younger generations to know and love God's Word is by challenging their parents and grandparents to know and love God's Word. Thank God for the marvelous opportunity to influence children, even those not yet born, to put their trust in God. Use Psalm 78:1-7 as a guideline to pray for wisdom to carry out this awesome duty.

Before the Session:

1. Secure a yardstick or ruler.
2. Prepare the following handout: Group 1: Read "The Correction Factor" in Day 2. Read Proverbs 4:1-27 and note verses that speak about the early correction and training of children. Be prepared to present what you have learned to the class. Group 2: Read "The Communication Factor" in Day 2. Read Proverbs 4:1-27 and note verses that speak about communicating with children. Be prepared to present what you have learned to the class. Group 3: Read "The Conversion Factor" in Day 2. Read Proverbs 4:1-27 and note verses that speak about helping children experience salvation and eternal life. Be prepared to present what you have learned to the class.

During the Session:

1. Ask: *As you grew up, did you turn away from some things your parents taught you? Was that a good or bad decision? Have you once again accepted some of those teachings you rejected earlier? Why?* OR Display a yardstick. Ask how it can be used positively and negatively. Ask how the Ten Commandments are like a yardstick. (provides a standard) Ask the class to state some of the many ways the Ten Commandments can be used positively in raising children. Declare: *We must be careful not to use the Ten Commandments in a negative way. We must not beat children over the head with the Law or hold the commandments up to show our kids how they don't measure up. Proverbs 22:6 presents four positive ways to teach children to live by God's standards.* AFTER EITHER OPTION Read Proverbs 22:6. Discuss the second activity in Day 1. (At this point in the class session you may want to present the material from Day 5 about what this verse does and does not say, especially if there are parents in your class who are struggling with straying children.)
2. Organize the class into three groups and distribute the handouts from "Before the Session" #2 (above) to each group. Give them several moments to complete their assignments. Allow groups to

Week of JULY 17

share. Ask: *How closely would you say this father's desire for his son matches your desire for your children? Which verses in Proverbs 4 speak to your desire for your children at this point in their lives? How can we get our children to listen to us so our earnest desires for them can be realized?* Remark that parents must correct with consistency if they want their children to listen and obey.

3. Ask if participants have ever heard others say they don't want to teach values to their children so the children can be free to choose their own beliefs and values. Ask, *What would happen if they took care of their yards the way they raise their children?* (grow wild, overgrown with weeds) Comment, *Gardens and children can only flourish if they are cared for with loving discipline.* Instruct learners to listen for truths about discipline as you read aloud Hebrews 12:5-11. Call for responses and write them on the board. Ask how those truths listed on the board can encourage parents to consistently correct their children. Invite volunteers to state additional reasons from Day 3 that parents must discipline their children.

4. Review the seven rules for discipline from Day 3. Avoid a debate about spanking. Instead, focus on how to consistently, lovingly discipline children. Discuss the final activity in Day 3. Invite someone to read 2 Corinthians 7:8-11. Compare kinds of discipline that cause worldly and godly grief. Discuss how parents can discern if their children are experiencing sorrow that leads to repentance and how to support children as they make necessary changes. Ask, *What if parents didn't start early enough—how can they still apply these seven rules?*

5. Comment that Proverbs 22:6 also encourages parents to communicate with creativity. The class has discussed many creative ways for teaching children the Ten Commandments over the course of this study. Allow volunteers to share which creative methods have inspired them and which ones they have begun to put into practice. (If the majority of your class is not involved in daily child-rearing, invite learners to share how this study has challenged them to live in obedience to the Ten Commandments and to influence others to do the same.)

6. Close in prayer.

NOTES

ABOUT THE WRITERS

John MacArthur

one of today's foremost Bible teachers, is the author of numerous bestselling books that have touched millions of lives. He is pastor-teacher of Grace Community Church in Sun Valley, California, and president of The Master's College and Seminary. He is also president of Grace to You, the ministry that produces the internationally syndicated radio program *Grace to You* and a host of print, audio, and Internet resources—all featuring John's popular, verse-by-verse teaching. He also authored the notes in *The MacArthur Study Bible,* which has been awarded the Gold Medallion and has sold more than 500,000 copies. John and his wife, Patricia, have four grown children and twelve grandchildren.

For more details about John MacArthur and all his Bible-teaching resources, contact Grace to You at 800-55-GRACE or *www.gty.org*.

AMY SUMMERS wrote the personal learning activities and teaching plans for this study.

ABOUT THIS STUDY

Read Matthew 10:2-4 in your Bible. In the space provided list the names of the twelve apostles. Draw a star by the name of the apostle who fascinates you the most. Check the names of those apostles you would like to learn more about.

1. _____ 2. _____

3. _____ 4. _____

5. _____ 6. _____

7. _____ 8. _____

9. _____ 10. _____

11. _____ 12. _____

Twelve Ordinary Men

I have always been fascinated with the lives of the twelve apostles. The personality types of these men are familiar to us. They are just like us, and they are like other people we know. They were perfectly ordinary men in every way. Not one of them was renowned for scholarship or great erudition. They were all too prone to mistakes, misstatements, wrong attitudes, lapses of faith, and bitter failure—no one more so than the leader of the group, Peter. They spanned the political spectrum. At least four, and possibly seven, were fishermen and close friends from Capernaum. Most of them were from Galilee, an agricultural region at the intersection of trade routes. And Galilee remained their home base for most of Jesus' ministry—not (as some might think) Jerusalem in Judea, which was the political and religious capital of Israel.

Yet with all their faults and character flaws—as remarkably ordinary as they were—these men carried on a ministry after Jesus' ascension that left an indelible impact on the world. Their ministry continues to influence us even today. God graciously empowered and used these men to inaugurate the spread of the gospel message and to turn the world upside down (Acts 17:6). Ordinary men—people like you and me—became the instruments by which Christ's message was carried to the ends of the earth. No wonder they are such fascinating characters.

John MacArthur

John MacARTHUR

The Apostle with the Foot-Shaped Mouth

"Simon . . . also named Peter"

We have four lists of the twelve apostles in the New Testament: Matthew 10:2–4; Mark 3:16–19; Luke 6:13–16; and Acts 1:13. The first name in all four lists is Peter. He thus stands out as the leader. We also have the explicit statement of Matthew 10:2: "Now the names of the twelve apostles are these: first, Simon, who is called Peter." The word translated "first" in that verse is the Greek term *protos*. It doesn't refer to the first in a list; it speaks of the chief, the leader of the group. Peter's leadership is further evident in the way he normally acts as spokesman for the whole group. He is always in the foreground, taking the lead. He seems to have had a naturally dominant personality, and the Lord put it to good use among the Twelve.

Simon was a very common name. There are at least seven Simons in the Gospel accounts alone. Among the Twelve were two named Simon (Simon Peter and Simon the Zealot). Our Simon's full name at birth was Simon Bar-Jonah (Matthew 16:17), meaning "Simon, son of Jonah" (John 21:15–17). Simon Peter's father's name, then, was John (sometimes rendered Jonas or Jonah). We know nothing more about his parents.

Simon Peter was a fisherman by trade. He and his brother Andrew were heirs to a family fishing business, centered in Capernaum. They caught fish on the Sea of Galilee. Simon Peter had a wife. We know this because in Luke 4:38 Jesus healed his mother-in-law and the Apostle Paul said in 1 Corinthians 9:5 that Peter took his wife on his apostolic mission.

The Lord gave Simon another name. Luke introduces him this way: "Simon, whom He [Jesus] also named Peter" (Luke 6:14). Luke's choice of

---

Apostle—"One who is sent." *(Holman Bible Dictionary)*

The term *apostle* used in this study refers to the twelve men Jesus chose to train for the task of carrying His message to the world.

Week of JULY 24

words here is important. Jesus didn't merely give him a new name to replace the old one; He "also" named him Peter. This disciple was known sometimes as Simon, sometimes as Peter, and sometimes as Simon Peter.

"Peter" was a sort of nickname. It means "Rock." (*Petros* is the Greek word for "a piece of rock, a stone.") The Aramaic equivalent was *Cephas* (see 1 Corinthians 1:12; 3:22; 9:5; 15:5; Galatians 2:9). John 1:42 describes Jesus' first face-to-face meeting with Simon Peter: "Now when Jesus looked at him, He said, 'You are Simon the son of Jonah. You shall be called Cephas' (which is translated, A Stone)." Those were apparently the first words Jesus ever said to Peter. And from then on, "Rock" was his nickname.

The nickname was significant, and the Lord had a specific reason for choosing it. By nature Simon was brash, vacillating, and undependable. He tended to make great promises he couldn't follow through with. Jesus changed Simon's name, it appears, because He wanted the nickname to be a perpetual reminder to him about who he *should* be. And from that point on, whatever Jesus called him sent him a subtle message. If Jesus called him Simon, Jesus was signaling him that he was acting like his old self.

Read the following passages in your Bible and fill in each blank to complete the statement.

1. Luke 22:31-34. Jesus called Peter "Simon" right before He foretold Peter's _____.

2. Mark 14:32-38. Jesus called Peter "Simon" when Peter _____.

After the resurrection, Jesus instructed His disciples to return to Galilee, where He planned to appear to them (Matthew 28:7). Impatient Simon apparently got tired of waiting, so he announced that he was going back to fishing (John 21:3). As usual, the other disciples dutifully followed their leader. They fished all night and caught nothing. Jesus met them on the shore the following morning, where He had prepared breakfast for them. Three times Jesus addressed Peter as Simon and asked, "Simon, son of Jonah, do you love Me?" (John 21:15–17). Three times, Peter affirmed his love. That was the last time Jesus ever had to call him Simon.

Peter's name is mentioned in the Gospels more than any other name except Jesus. No one speaks as often as Peter, and no one is spoken to by the Lord as often as Peter. No disciple is so frequently rebuked by the Lord as Peter; and no disciple ever rebukes the Lord except Peter (Matthew 16:22). No one else confessed Christ more boldly or acknowledged His lordship more explicitly; yet no other disciple ever verbally denied Christ as forcefully or as publicly as Peter did. No one is praised and blessed by Christ the way Peter was; yet Peter was also the only one Christ ever addressed as Satan. The Lord had harsher things to say to Peter than He ever said to any of the others.

Peter was exactly like most Christians—both carnal and spiritual. He succumbed to the habits of the flesh sometimes; he functioned in the Spirit other times. He was sinful sometimes, but other times he acted the way a righteous man ought to act. This vacillating man—sometimes Simon, sometimes Peter—was the leader of the Twelve.

Read John 1:42 in your Bible. Personalize Jesus' words to Peter by filling in the first blank with qualities you possess now and the second blank with qualities you believe the Lord wants to develop in you.

"You are _____.

You will be _____."

The Raw Material

Raw material of a good leader:

1. Inquisitiveness

Whom do you know who possesses this quality?

_____

How does inquisitiveness make him or her a good leader?

_____

We see in Peter's life three key elements that go into the making of a true leader. The first element is *the right raw material*—certain rather obvious features in Simon Peter's natural disposition that were critical to his leadership ability. These are not generally characteristics that can be developed merely by training; they were innate features of Peter's temperament.

Week of JULY 24

The first one is *inquisitiveness*. When you're looking for a leader, you want someone who asks lots of questions. People who are not inquisitive simply don't make good leaders. Curiosity is crucial to leadership. People who are content with what they don't know, happy to remain ignorant about what they don't understand, complacent about what they haven't analyzed, and comfortable living with problems they haven't solved—such people cannot lead. Leaders need to have an insatiable curiosity.

In the Gospel accounts, Peter asks more questions than all the other apostles combined. It was usually Peter who asked the Lord to explain His difficult sayings (Matthew 15:15; Luke 12:41). It was Peter who asked how often he needed to forgive (Matthew 18:21). It was Peter who asked what reward the disciples would get for having left everything to follow Jesus (Matthew 19:27). It was Peter who asked about the withered fig tree (Mark 11:21). It was Peter who asked questions of the risen Christ (John 21:20–22). He always wanted to know more, to understand better.

Another necessary ingredient is *initiative.* Someone wired for leadership will have drive, ambition, and energy. A true leader must be the kind of person who makes things happen, a starter. Notice that Peter not only *asked* questions; he was also usually the first one to *answer* any question posed by Christ.

There was that famous occasion when Jesus asked, "Who do men say that I, the Son of Man, am?" (Matthew 16:13). Several opinions were circulating among the people about that. "So they said, 'Some say John the Baptist, some Elijah, and others Jeremiah or one of the prophets'" (v. 14). Jesus then asked the disciples in particular, "But who do *you* say that I am?" (v. 15, emphasis added). It was at that point that Peter boldly spoke out above the rest: "You are the Christ, the Son of the living God" (v. 16). The other disciples were still processing the question, but Peter was bold and decisive. Yes, sometimes he had to take a step back, undo, retract, or be rebuked. But the fact that he was always willing to grab opportunity by the throat marked him as a natural leader.

In the Garden of Gethsemane, when Roman soldiers from Fort Antonia came to arrest Jesus, all three synoptic Gospel writers say there was a "great multitude" armed with "with swords and staves" (Matthew 26:47; see also Mark 14:43; Luke 22:47). Without hesitating, Peter pulled out his sword and took a swing at the head of Malchus, the servant of the high priest. But Peter was a fisherman, not a swordsman. Malchus ducked, and

2. Initiative

Whom do you know who possesses this quality?

_____

How does initiative make him or her a good leader?

_____

his ear was severed. So Jesus "touched his ear and healed him" (Luke 22:51). Then He told Peter, "Put your sword in its place, for all who take the sword will perish by the sword" (Matthew 26:52).

Think about that incident. What did Peter think he was going to do? Behead all the multitude, one by one? Sometimes in Peter's passion for taking the initiative, he overlooked the obvious big-picture realities.

But with all his brashness, Peter had the raw material from which a leader could be made. Better to work with a man like that than to try to motivate someone who is always passive and hesitant. As the familiar saying goes, it is much easier to tone down a fanatic than to resurrect a corpse. Some people have to be dragged tediously in any forward direction. Not Peter. He always wanted to move ahead. He wanted to know what he didn't know. He wanted to understand what he didn't understand. He was the first to ask questions and the first to try to answer questions. He was a man who always took the initiative, seized the moment, and charged ahead. That's the stuff of leadership.

There's a third element of the raw material that makes a true leader: _involvement._ True leaders are always in the middle of the action. They do not sit in the background telling everyone else what to do while they live a life of comfort away from the fray. A true leader goes through life with a cloud of dust around him. That is precisely why people _follow_ him. The true leader must show the way. He goes before his followers.

Jesus came to the disciples one night out in the middle of the Sea of Galilee, walking on the water in the midst of a violent storm. Who out of all the disciples jumped out of the boat? Peter. The other disciples wondered if they were seeing a ghost (Matthew 14:26). But Peter said, "Lord, if it is You, command me to come to You on the water." Jesus answered, "Come" (vv. 27–28)—and before anyone knew it, Peter was out of the boat, walking on the water. The rest of the disciples were still clinging to their seats, trying to make sure they didn't fall overboard in the storm. But Peter was out of the boat. That's involvement—_serious_ involvement.

Similarly, although Peter denied Christ, he and one other disciple were the only ones who followed Jesus to the high priest's house to see what would become of Jesus (John 18:15). And in the courtyard of the high priest's house, Peter was the only one close enough for Jesus to turn and look him in the eyes when the rooster crowed (Luke 22:61). Long after the other disciples had forsaken Christ and fled in fear for their lives, Peter

---

3. Involvement

Whom do you know who possesses this quality?

_____

How does involvement make him or her a good leader?

_____

Week of JULY 24

was virtually alone in a position where such a temptation could snare him, because despite his fear and weakness, he couldn't abandon Christ completely. He had a passion to be personally involved, so he was always found close to the heart of the action. That's the sign of a true leader.

Such was the raw fabric of which Peter was made: an insatiable inquisitiveness, a willingness to take the initiative, and a passion to be personally involved. Now it was up to the Lord to train and shape him, because frankly, that kind of raw material, if not submitted to the Lord's control, can be downright dangerous.

What is your raw material? _____

How are you allowing God to mold and reshape that material so it's useful to Him? _____

Life Experiences

How did the Lord take a man cut from such rough fabric and refine him into a leader? For one thing, he made sure Peter had the kind of life experiences that formed him into the kind of leader Christ wanted him to be.

Experience can be a hard teacher. In Peter's case the ups and downs of his experience were dramatic and often painful. His life was filled with tortuous zigs and zags. The Lord dragged him through three years of tests and difficulties that gave him a lifetime of the kind of experiences every true leader must endure.

The apostle Peter learned a lot through hard experience. He learned, for example, that crushing defeat and deep humiliation often follow hard on the heels of our greatest victories. Just after Christ commended him for his great confession in Matthew 16:16 ("You are the Christ, the Son of the living God"), Peter suffered the harshest rebuke ever recorded of a disciple in the New Testament.

Read Matthew 16:17,23 in your Bible and fill in the blanks.

One minute Jesus called Peter b_____.

In the next paragraph He called Peter S_____.

Through the painful experience of being rebuked by the Lord, Peter learned that he was vulnerable to Satan. Satan could fill his mouth just as surely as the Lord could fill it. If Peter minded the things of men rather than the things of God, or if he did not do the will of God, he could be an instrument of the enemy.

Later, Peter fell victim to Satan again on the night of Jesus' arrest. This time he learned the hard way that he was humanly weak and could not trust his own resolve. All his boasting promises and earnest resolutions did not keep him from falling. After declaring in front of everyone that he would *never* deny Christ, he denied Him anyway, and he punctuated his denials with passionate curses. Satan was sifting him as wheat. Thus Peter learned how much chaff and how little substance there was in him and how watchful and careful he must be to rely only on the Lord's strength. At the same time, he learned that in spite of his own sinful tendencies and spiritual weaknesses, the Lord wanted to use him and would sustain him and preserve him no matter what.

All those things Peter learned by experience. Sometimes the experiences were bitter, distressing, humiliating, and painful. Other times they were encouraging, uplifting, and perfectly glorious—such as when Peter saw Christ's divine brilliance on the Mount of Transfiguration. Either way, Peter made the most of his experiences, gleaning from them lessons that helped make him the great leader he became.

Identify a recent positive or negative personal experience. _____

How can that experience help you be a more effective leader for the Lord? _____

Week of JULY 24

Character Qualities (Part 1)

Three elements in the making of a leader:

1. Raw Material

2. Life Experiences

3. Character Qualities

A third element in the making of a leader is the right character. What are some of the character qualities of a spiritual leader that Christ developed in Peter?

One is *submission*. At first glance that may seem an unusual quality to cultivate in a leader. After all, the leader is the person in charge, and he expects other people to submit to him, right? But a true leader doesn't just demand submission; he is an example of submission by the way he submits to the Lord and to His Word—and to those in authority over him.

Leaders tend to be confident and aggressive. They naturally dominate. Peter had that tendency in him. He was quick to speak and quick to act. As we have seen, he was a man of initiative. That means he was always inclined to try to take control of every situation. In order to balance that side of him, the Lord taught him submission.

One classic example concerns the temple tax in Matthew 17:24–27. It's intriguing that the miracle Jesus worked demonstrated His absolute *sovereignty*, and yet at the same time, He was being an example of human *submission*. If Jesus was Lord over nature to such a degree, He certainly had authority as God's Son to opt out of the temple tax. And yet He taught Peter by example how to submit willingly.

Submission is an indispensible character quality for leaders to cultivate. If they would teach people to submit, they must be examples of submission themselves. And sometimes a leader must submit even when there might seem to be very good arguments against submitting. Peter learned the lesson well.

A second character quality Peter learned was *restraint*. Self-control, discipline, moderation, and reserve don't necessarily come naturally to someone who lives life at the head of the pack. That is why so many leaders have problems with anger and out-of-control passions. Hotheadedness goes naturally with the sort of active, decisive, initiative-taking personality that makes one a leader in the first place. Such a man easily grows impatient with people who lack vision or who underperform. He can be quickly irritated by those who throw up obstacles to success. Therefore he must learn restraint in order to be a good leader.

That scene in the garden in Matthew 26:47–56 where Peter tried to decapitate Malchus is a classic example of his natural lack of restraint. Jesus immediately healed the damage and rebuked Peter sternly. That rebuke must have been especially difficult for Peter, coming as it did in front of a horde of enemies. But Peter learned much from what he witnessed that night.

Peter also had to learn *humility*. Leaders are often tempted by the sin of pride. In fact, the besetting sin of leadership may be the tendency to think more of oneself than one ought to think. When people are following your lead, constantly praising you, looking up to you, and admiring you, it is too easy to be overcome with pride.

We can observe in Peter a tremendous amount of self-confidence. It is obvious by the way he jumps in with answers to all the questions. It is obvious in most of his actions, such as when he stepped out of the boat and began to walk on water. It became obvious in the worst and most disastrous way on that fateful occasion in Matthew 26:31 when Jesus foretold that His disciples would forsake Him. Peter was cocksure: "Even if all are made to stumble because of You, I will *never* be made to stumble" (v. 33, emphasis added). Then he added, "Lord, I am ready to go with You, both to prison and to death" (Luke 22:33).

Of course, as usual, Peter was wrong and Jesus was right. Peter *did* deny Christ not once, but multiple times, just as Jesus had warned. But the Lord used all of this to make Peter humble. Humility became one of the virtues that characterized Peter's life, his message, and his leadership style.

> **We discover from letters Peter wrote later in life that he learned his lessons well. Read the following passages and draw a line to match the reference with the character quality Peter allowed the Lord to build into his life.**
>
> | | |
> |---|---|
> | 1 Peter 2:13-18 | Humility |
> | 1 Peter 2:21-23 | Submission |
> | 1 Peter 5:5-6 | Restraint |

Week of JULY 24

Character Qualities (Part 2)

Peter also learned *love*. True spiritual leadership means loving service to one another. The real leader is someone who serves, not someone who demands to be waited upon.

This is a hard lesson for many natural leaders to learn. They tend to see people as a means to their end. Leaders are usually task-oriented rather than people-oriented. And so they often use people, or plow over people, in order to achieve their goals. But the true leader loves and serves those whom he leads.

The Lord Himself constantly modeled loving servant-leadership for the disciples. Nowhere is it more plainly on display than in the Upper Room on the night of His betrayal. After Judas had left, Jesus told the eleven, "A new commandment I give to you, that you love one another; as I have loved you, that you also love one another. By this all will know that you are My disciples, if you have love for one another" (John 13:34–35). How had He loved them? He washed their feet. While they were arguing about who was the greatest, He showed them what loving, humble service for one another looks like.

It's hard for most leaders to stoop and wash the feet of those whom they perceive as subordinates. But that was the example of leadership Jesus gave, and He urged His disciples to follow it. In fact, He told them that showing love to one another in such a way is the mark of a true disciple.

Did Peter learn to love? He certainly did. Love became one of the hallmarks of his teaching. In 1 Peter 4:8 he wrote, "Above all things have fervent love for one another, for 'love will cover a multitude of sins.'" The Greek word translated "fervent" in that verse is *ektenes*, literally meaning "stretched to the limit." Peter was urging us to love to the maximum of our capacity. The love he spoke of is not about a feeling. It's not about how we respond to people who are naturally lovable.

**Paraphrase
1 Peter 4:8 in your own words:**

101

It's about a love that covers and compensates for others' failures and weaknesses: "Love will cover a multitude of sins." Peter had learned that lesson from Christ's example.

Another important character quality Peter needed to learn was <u>compassion.</u> When the Lord warned Peter that he would deny Him, He said, "Satan has asked for you, that he may sift you as wheat" (Luke 22:31). Wheat was typically separated from the chaff by being shaken and tossed up into the air in a stiff wind. The chaff was blown away and the wheat would fall into a pile, thus purified.

We might have expected Jesus to reassure Peter by saying, "I'm not going to allow Satan to sift you." But He didn't. He essentially let Peter know that He had given Satan the permission he sought. He would allow the Devil to put Peter to the test. Jesus said, in essence, "I'm going to let him do it. I'm going to let Satan shake the very foundations of your life. Then I'm going to let him toss you to the wind—until there's nothing left but the reality of your faith." Jesus did reassure Peter that the apostle's faith would survive the ordeal. "I have prayed for you," Jesus told him, "that your faith should not fail; and when you have returned to Me, strengthen your brethren" (v. 32).

What was this all about? Jesus was equipping Peter to strengthen the brethren. People with natural leadership abilities often tend to be short on compassion, lousy comforters, and impatient with others. They don't stop very long to care for the wounded as they pursue their goals. Peter needed to learn compassion through his own ordeal, so that when it was over, he could strengthen others in theirs.

For the rest of his life, Peter would need to show compassion to people who were struggling. After being sifted by Satan, Peter was well equipped to empathize with others' weaknesses. In 1 Peter 5:8–10, he wrote, "Be sober, be vigilant; because your adversary the devil walks about like a roaring lion, seeking whom he may devour. Resist him, steadfast in the faith, knowing that the same sufferings are experienced by your brotherhood in the world. But may the God of all grace, who called us to His eternal glory by Christ Jesus, after you have suffered a while, perfect, establish, strengthen, and settle you."

Finally, Peter had to learn <u>courage.</u> Not the impetuous, headlong, false kind of "courage" that caused him to swing his sword so wildly at Malchus, but <u>a mature, settled, intrepid willingness to suffer for Christ's</u>

Week of JULY 24

sake. The price of preaching would be death for Peter. He would need rock-solid courage to persevere.

You can practically see the birth of real courage in Peter's heart at Pentecost, when he was filled and empowered by the Holy Spirit. Notice Peter's and John's courage in the events of Acts 4:1–22 when they were brought before the Sanhedrin. Soon, however, they were brought back before the Sanhedrin for continuing to preach. Again Peter showed rock-solid courage (Acts 5:29).

Read Acts 5:29 in the margin. Name an experience when you courageously did things God's way rather than the popular way.

_____

_____

"But Peter and the apostles replied, 'We must obey God rather than men'" (Acts 5:29, HCSB).

How did Peter's life end? We know that Jesus told Peter he would die as a martyr (John 21:18–19). Eusebius cites the testimony of Clement, who says that before Peter was crucified he was forced to watch the crucifixion of his own wife. When it was Peter's turn to die, he pleaded to be crucified upside down because he wasn't worthy to die as his Lord had died. Thus he was nailed to a cross head-downward.

How did your study of the Apostle Peter:

Encourage you? _____

_____

Challenge you? _____

_____

NOTES

To the Leader:

Read 1 Peter 1:22 in your Bible. How do you demonstrate to the learners in your class that you love them deeply and earnestly? Ask the Lord to empower you to be pure and obedient to His Word so you can honestly say—and show—that you love others sincerely.

Before the Session

1. Prayerfully choose the teaching steps and learning activities from Week 1 that you will incorporate into your teaching plan.
2. Make a list of nicknames of famous persons (for the optional Step 1 activity). (Find some at *www.westward.com/club.trivia22.htm*.)

During the Session

1. Encourage learners to name qualities of a good leader. Write responses on the board. Discuss why those qualities make a good leader. Write *impetuous, brash, uneducated,* and *wishy-washy* on the board. Ask if those qualities describe a good leader and why. Comment that those are words that describe Simon Peter's human nature. Today you will observe how Jesus transformed Peter into the leader of the apostles. OR Encourage learners to state nicknames of famous persons and tell how the persons received those nicknames. (Be prepared to share some persons nicknames to get the discussion rolling.) Invite volunteers to share their own nicknames and how they got them. Comment that nicknames often reveal some aspect of a person's character. Today you will see how the apostle Simon Peter's character was transformed to reflect the qualities of the nickname Jesus gave him.

2. Invite a volunteer to read John 1:35-42. Ask how Jesus could give Simon a nickname when He'd never met him before. From Day 1, explore the meaning of the name *Peter*. Refer to the Scriptures in the first activity in Day 1 and ask: *Does this man seem more like shifting sand or a solid rock? Why? Do you think Jesus was stating a present or future reality when he gave Simon the name Peter? How might his new name have inspired Simon to be more rock-like?* (If most adults in your class are parents, you might want to explore the value of positive expectations in raising children.)

3. From Day 2 ask learners to state the three ingredients from Peter's natural disposition that were crucial to his leadership. Ask who we normally expect to be curious. State: *Next to "no" the most common word spoken by a child is "Why?"* Ask why adults must also be inquisitive.

Week of JULY 24

Request someone read Matthew 18:3-4. Discuss why curiosity is essential to strong leadership. Ask three volunteers to read aloud Peter's questions from Matthew 15:15; 18:21; and John 21:20-22. Ask: *Do you think the apostles were glad Peter asked questions? Why? Do you think they got tired of Peter's questions? Why? Do you think that would have stopped Peter from asking questions? Why? Do you think Jesus got tired of Peter's questions? Why?* (Jesus always answered Peter's questions!)

4. Use Dr. MacArthur's comments and the biblical accounts in Day 2 to explore how Simon's negative qualities of brashness and impetuousness could be transformed into leadership qualities of initiative and involvement. Request learners silently consider the final activity of Day 2. Guide the class to name raw materials in persons' dispositions, such as sensitivity, passion, and charisma. Discuss how those traits can be dangerous if not submitted to God and how they can be useful when they are submitted to God. Guide the class to explore how they can allow God to mold and shape their raw material.

5. Invite a volunteer to read Matthew 16:13-23. Ask why Jesus called Peter "blessed" and soon after called Simon "Satan." Discuss how Peter must have felt after both instances. Explore what Peter learned from that up-and-down experience and how that made him a better leader.

6. Discuss character qualities of leaders and their accompanying biblical illustrations from Days 4 and 5. You probably won't have time to discuss all of them in-depth. Allow the Spirit to guide your discussion to focus on those character qualities your class most needs to explore. To explore the quality of courage invite three volunteers to read Mark 14:66-71; Acts 2:14; and 4:18-20. Ask, *What made the difference in Peter's courage?* For insight on answering that question ask someone to read John 21:15-19. Point out this was the last time Jesus called Peter "Simon." Ask how this experience strengthened Peter's courage. Remark that every good leadership quality must flow out of a rock-solid love for and commitment to Jesus.

7. Allow volunteers to share their responses to the final activity of Day 5.

8. Close in prayer, asking that each person will allow Jesus to shape who they are now into who He wants them to become.

NOTES

John **MacARTHUR**

The Apostle of Small Things

day One

Andrew, the Manly Man

Complete the sentence below to reflect how you are often identified.

_____ (your name), _____'s brother/sister/mother/father/wife/husband.

How do you feel about that identification?

_____

Peter and his brother Andrew had probably been lifelong companions with the other set of fishermen—brothers from Capernaum—James and John, the sons of Zebedee. The four of them apparently shared common spiritual interests even before they met Christ. They evidently visited the wilderness where John the Baptist was preaching and became his disciples. That is where they were when they first met Christ. And when they returned to fishing (before Jesus called them to be full-time disciples), they remained together as partners. So it was quite natural that this little group formed a cohesive unit within the Twelve.

Of the four in the inner circle, however, Andrew was the least conspicuous. Scripture doesn't tell us a lot about him. You can practically count on your fingers the number of times he is mentioned specifically in the Gospels. (In fact, apart from the places where all twelve disciples are listed, Andrew's name appears in the New Testament only nine times, and most of those references simply mention him in passing.) Andrew lived his life in the shadow of his better-known brother. Many of the verses that name him add that he was Peter's brother.

Week of JULY 31

Andrew's name means "manly," and it seems a fitting description. Remember that when Jesus met him for the first time, Andrew was already a devout man who had joined the ranks of John the Baptist's disciples.

Read Matthew 3:1-7 in your Bible. What hints about Andrew do you gain from this glimpse of John the Baptist?

_____

The Baptist was well known for his rugged appearance and his spartan lifestyle. He lived and ministered in the wilderness, cut off from all the comforts and conveniences of city life. To follow John the Baptist as a disciple, one could hardly be soft.

If you desire to dig deeper...

Read John 1:19-37 in your Bible. What do you admire about John the Baptist?

_____

_____

_____

Meeting and Following Jesus

Chapter 1 of John's Gospel describes Andrew's first meeting with Jesus. It took place in the wilderness, where John the Baptist was preaching repentance and baptizing converts. Andrew's personal encounter with Jesus took place the day after Jesus' baptism (vv. 29–34). Andrew and John were standing next to the Baptist when Jesus walked by and John the Baptist said, "Behold the Lamb of God!" (vv. 35–36). They immediately left John's side and began to follow Jesus (v. 37). Don't imagine that they were being fickle or untrue to their mentor. Quite the opposite. John the Baptist had already expressly denied that he was the Messiah (vv. 19–20). John had already said in the most plain and forthright terms that he was only the forerunner of the Messiah. He had come to prepare the way and to point people in the right direction (v. 23). Andrew and John therefore had expectations of a coming Messiah, waiting only for the right person to be identified. That is why as soon as they heard John the Baptist identify Christ as the Lamb of God, the two disciples left John to follow Christ. The two men asked Jesus where He was staying and then spent the remainder of that day with Him (vv. 38–39). They left convinced that they had found the true Messiah. They met, became acquainted with, and began to be taught by Jesus that very day. Thus Andrew and John became Jesus' first disciples.

> **Read John 1:41-42 in your Bible. What is the first thing Andrew did after he met Jesus? (check one)**
> ❑ **Sought admiration from the community for finding the Messiah.**
> ❑ **Begged to stay with Jesus as His number one disciple.**
> ❑ **Brought his brother to Jesus.**

The news was too good to keep to himself, so Andrew went and found his brother—whom he wanted to know Jesus—and he led him to Christ.

Andrew and Peter went back to Capernaum and continued their fishing career after that initial meeting with Christ. It was at a later time—perhaps several months later—that Jesus came to Galilee to minister. Jesus had begun His ministry in and around Jerusalem. But then He returned to Galilee to preach and heal, and He eventually came to Capernaum. There He encountered the four brothers again, while they were fishing. Matthew 4:18–22 records that encounter. This was when they left fishing for a more permanent, full-time discipleship.

The Value of Individuals

When it came to dealing with people, Andrew fully appreciated the value of a single soul. He was known for bringing individuals, not crowds, to Jesus. Almost every time we see him in the Gospel accounts, he is bringing someone to Jesus.

Remember his first act after discovering Christ was to go and get Peter. That incident set the tone for Andrew's style of ministry. At the feeding of

Week of JULY 31

the five thousand, for example, it was Andrew who brought the boy with the loaves and fishes to Christ. All the other disciples were at a loss to know how to obtain food for the multitude. It was Andrew who took the young boy to Jesus and said, "There is a lad here who has five barley loaves and two small fish" (John 6:9).

> **Read John 12:20-22 in your Bible. Fill in the blanks to diagram the progression that occurs in this passage.**
>
> G_____ came to P_____ who took them
>
> to A_____ who led them to J_____.

It is significant that these men approached Philip, but Philip took the men to Andrew and let Andrew introduce them to the Master. Andrew was not confused when people wanted to see Jesus. He simply brought them to Him. He understood that Jesus would want to meet anyone who wanted to meet Him (see John 6:37).

"Everyone the Father gives Me will come to Me, and the one who comes to Me I will never cast out" (John 6:37, HCSB).

Andrew was obviously poised and comfortable introducing people to Christ, because he did it so often. He apparently knew Jesus well and had no insecurities about bringing others to Him. One thing I have observed in all my years of ministry is that the most effective and important aspects of evangelism usually take place on an individual, personal level. Most people do not come to Christ as an immediate response to a sermon they hear in a crowded setting. They come to Christ because of the influence of an individual.

Both Andrew and his brother Peter had evangelistic hearts, but their methods were dramatically different. Peter preached at Pentecost, and three thousand people were added to the church. Nothing in Scripture indicates that Andrew ever preached to a crowd or stirred masses of people. But remember that it was he who brought Peter to Christ. In the sovereign providence of God, Andrew's act of faithfulness in bringing his own brother to Christ was the individual act that led to the conversion of the man who would preach that great sermon at Pentecost. All the fruit of Peter's ministry is ultimately also the fruit of Andrew's faithful, individual witness.

God often works that way. Few have ever heard of Edward Kimball. His name is a footnote in the annals of church history. But he was the Sunday School teacher who led D. L. Moody to Christ. He went one afternoon to

Record the name of one person you are seeking to introduce to Jesus.

_____

Identify ways you are ministering to this person:

_____

_____

_____

the Boston shoe store where the nineteen-year-old Moody was working, cornered him in the stockroom, and introduced him to Christ.

Of course, D. L. Moody was used mightily by the Lord as an evangelist. His ministry made a massive impact on both sides of the Atlantic, spanning most of the second half of the nineteenth century. Tens of thousands testified that they came to Christ because of his ministry. Moody subsequently founded Moody Bible Institute, where thousands of missionaries, evangelists, and other Christian workers have been trained during the past century and sent out into all the world. All of that began when one man was faithful to introduce another individual to Christ.

That's the way Andrew usually seemed to minister: one-on-one. Most pastors would love to have their churches populated by people with Andrew's mentality. Too many Christians think that because they can't speak in front of groups or because they don't have leadership gifts, they aren't responsible to evangelize. There are few who, like Andrew, understand the value of befriending just one person and bringing him or her to Christ.

day four

The Value of Insignificant Gifts

Some people see the big picture more clearly just because they appreciate the value of small things. Andrew fits that category. This comes through clearly in John's account of the feeding of the five thousand.

Jesus had gone to a mountain to try to be alone with His disciples. As often happened when He took a break from public ministry, the clamoring multitudes tracked Him down.

Suddenly a huge throng of people approached. Somehow they had discovered where Jesus was. It was nearing time to eat, and bread would be the object lesson in the message Jesus would preach to the multitude. So He made it clear that He wanted to feed the multitude. He asked Philip where they might buy bread. John adds an editorial comment to stress the fact that Christ was sovereignly in control of these circumstances: "This He said to test him, for He Himself knew what He would do" (John 6:6).

Week of JULY 31

Philip did a quick accounting and determined that they had only two hundred denarii in their treasury. A denarius was a day's pay for a common laborer, so two hundred denarii would be approximately eight months' wages. It was a significant sum, but the crowd was so large that even two hundred denarii was inadequate to buy enough food for them. Philip's vision was overwhelmed by the size of the need. He and the other disciples were at a loss to know what to do. Matthew, recounting this same incident, reports that the disciples said, "This is a deserted place, and the hour is already late. Send the multitudes away, that they may go into the villages and buy themselves food" (Matthew 14:15). But Jesus answered, "They do not need to go away. You give them something to eat" (v. 16). The disciples must have been stymied by this. Jesus' demand seemed unreasonable.

At that point, Andrew spoke up. "There is a lad here who has five barley loaves and two small fish" (John 6:9). Of course, even Andrew knew that five barley loaves and two small fish would not be enough to feed five thousand people, but (in his typical fashion) he brought the boy to Jesus anyway. Jesus had commanded the disciples to feed the people, and Andrew knew He would not issue such a command without making it possible for them to obey. So Andrew did the best he could. He identified the one food source available, and he made sure Jesus knew about it. Something in him seemed to understand that no gift is insignificant in the hands of Jesus.

Read the rest of John's narrative in 6:10–13. What an amazing lesson! That so little could be used to accomplish so much was a testimony to the power of Christ. No gift is really insignificant in His hands.

Read Luke 21:1-4 in your Bible. What did Jesus teach His disciples? (check all that apply)

- ❑ Don't bother giving if you can't give a lot.
- ❑ The true measure of a gift's significance is the sacrificial faithfulness of the giver, not the size of the gift.
- ❑ You just have to give a little bit of what you own to God.
- ❑ God's ability to use a gift is in no way hindered or enhanced by the size of the gift.

Jesus taught that the poor person who gives everything he or she has is giving a greater gift than rich people who give much more out of their abundance. That's a difficult concept for the human mind to comprehend. But somehow Andrew seemed instinctively to know that he was not wasting Jesus' time by bringing such a paltry gift. It is not the greatness of the gift that counts but rather the greatness of the God to whom it is given. Andrew set the stage for the miracle.

Of course, Jesus didn't even need to have that boy's lunch in order to serve the crowd. He could have created food from nothing just as easily. But the way He fed the five thousand illustrates the way God always works. He takes the sacrificial and often insignificant gifts of people who give faithfully, and He multiplies them to accomplish monumental things.

What small gift or talent do you possess that seems to be of little value to Christ? _____

How will you sacrifice that possession to God today?

_____

day Five

The Value of Inconspicuous Service

Andrew is the very picture of all those who labor quietly in humble places, "not with eyeservice, as men-pleasers, but as bond-servants of Christ, doing the will of God from the heart" (Ephesians 6:6). He was not an impressive pillar like Peter, James, and John. He was a humbler stone. He was one of those rare people who is willing to take second place and to be in the place of support. He did not mind being hidden as long as the work was being done.

This is a lesson many Christians today would do well to learn. Scripture cautions against seeking roles of prominence. Jesus taught the disciples,

Week of JULY 31

"If any man desire to be first, the same shall be last of all, and servant of all" (Mark 9:35). It takes a special kind of person to be a leader with a servant's heart. Andrew was like that.

As far as we know, Andrew never preached to multitudes or founded any churches. He never wrote an epistle. He isn't mentioned in the Book of Acts or any of the epistles. Andrew is more a silhouette than a portrait on the pages of Scripture. In fact, the Bible does not record what happened to Andrew after Pentecost. Whatever role he played in early church history, he remained behind the scenes. Tradition says he took the gospel north. Eusebius, the early church historian, says Andrew went as far as Scythia. (That's why Andrew is the patron saint of Russia and also the patron saint of Scotland.) He was ultimately crucified in Achaia, which is in southern Greece, near Athens. One account says he led the wife of a provincial Roman governor to Christ, and that infuriated her husband. The governor demanded that his wife recant her devotion to Jesus Christ and she refused. So he had Andrew crucified.

By the governor's orders, those who crucified Andrew lashed him to his cross instead of nailing him, in order to prolong his sufferings. By most accounts, he hung on the cross for two days, exhorting passersby to turn to Christ for salvation. After a lifetime of ministry in the shadow of his more famous brother and in the service of His Lord, Andrew met a similar fate as theirs, remaining faithful and still endeavoring to bring people to Christ, right to the end.

Was he slighted? No. He was privileged. He was the first to hear that Jesus was the Lamb of God. He was the first to follow Christ. He was part of the inner circle, given intimate access to Christ. His name will be inscribed, along with the names of the other apostles, on the foundations of the eternal city—the New Jerusalem. Best of all, he had a whole lifetime of privilege, doing what he loved best—introducing individuals to his Lord.

Identify quiet servants in your church and indicate how will you express appreciation to them.

_____

_____

_____

What truths that you discovered about Andrew:

Encourage you? _____

_____

Challenge you? _____

_____

Amy SUMMERS

NOTES

To the Leader:

Carefully think about each learner in your class. What small gifts do they possess that they might think are of little use to God? Make an effort to affirm learners for the things they do for God's kingdom or for a character quality you admire in them. You may choose to do this through a face-to-face encounter or by a phone call, e-mail, or note.

Before the Session

1. Prepare one large and one small package. Wrap the large package in bright wrapping paper with a big bow. Wrap the small package in plain brown paper (for optional Step 1).
2. Provide thank-you cards for each learner.
3. Obtain a church directory with addresses of church members.

During the Session

1. Request that learners indicate whether they are the oldest, middle, youngest, or only child in their family. Invite volunteers to share advantages and disadvantages of their particular birth order. Ask: *Were you ever known as so-and-so's little brother or sister? How did you feel about that? Why?* Indicate that the Apostle Andrew is often identified as Peter's brother, yet he didn't try to grab a more prominent position. He chose to serve in the background. OR Display the large and small packages. Ask learners which package they would rather have and why. Ask which package draws the most attention. Inquire, *Judging from our study of Peter last week, which package would you say best represents him?* Comment that Peter's brother, Andrew, is better represented by the smaller plain package. Instead of resenting the fact he wasn't as attention-getting as his brother, Andrew quietly served Christ with his own gifts and personality.

2. Summarize John 1:35-40. Complete the activity in Day 2. Ask: *Do you think Andrew was tempted to keep this information to himself just so he could "have one over" on his brother for once? Why? What do you think motivated Andrew to tell Peter about Jesus—his love for his brother, his conviction Jesus is the Messiah, or something else entirely? Explain your answer.* Explain this was Andrew's and Peter's initial meeting with Jesus. Their calling to a deeper level of discipleship came later. Request someone read Matthew 4:18-22. Comment that people often think of this as the calling of Peter, James, and John while Andrew gets overlooked. Encourage the class to step into the background and look at this calling through Andrew's eyes. Ask: *Do you think Andrew*

Week of JULY 31

felt he received a call too or was he just tagging along with his brother? What reservations or fears do you think he might have had to follow Jesus? What motivated him to leave everything for Christ?

3. Discuss the activity in Day 3. Ask why learners think Philip approached Andrew instead of the other apostles when the Greeks asked to see Jesus. Discuss what qualities Andrew may have possessed that made him so approachable. Ask learners how they can develop some of those qualities in their own lives. Ask: *Do you think Peter was more valuable in God's kingdom than Andrew because he preached the gospel to thousands of people? Why or why not?* Use principles from Day 3 to add to the discussion. Invite volunteers to share the name of the person who led them to Christ. Allow volunteers to share the first name of someone they are seeking to introduce to Christ (margin activity in Day 3). Allow a time of silent prayer, prompting learners to thank God for the person who led them to Christ and asking for opportunities to share Christ with others.

4. Invite a volunteer to read John 6:1-13. Direct learners to estimate how many people were on the mountain that day. Ask: *How do you think Andrew was aware that one small boy in that large crowd had a sack lunch?* (You should focus the discussion on the fact that Andrew noticed individuals and appreciated the value of small things.) *What do you think Andrew learned about Jesus from this experience?* Request learners scan Matthew 14:13-21 and state what's missing in this account that was mentioned in John 6. (Andrew wasn't mentioned as the one who found the loaves and fish.) Ask: *Judging from what you know about Andrew, do you think he would mind that his name was left out? Why? What lessons can Christians learn from Andrew's example?* Ask someone to read Mark 9:35. Discuss the activity at the end of Day 5.

5. Ask learners to identify persons in your church who serve quietly in the background. Distribute thank-you cards and encourage learners to write a note of appreciation to one of those persons mentioned. Have a church directory on hand so learners can address their notes.

6. Close in prayer, thanking God for those who serve quietly and asking God to help the learners in your Bible study group to follow Andrew's example of quiet leadership.

NOTES

The Boanerges Brothers

James—The Apostle of Passion

If you desire to dig deeper...

Read Nehemiah 13:23-27 and answer the following:

How did Nehemiah act passionately?

Why did Nehemiah act so passionately?

How do Nehemiah's actions make you feel?

When do you think is the time and place for Nehemiah's type of fervent zeal?

Of the three disciples in Jesus' closest inner circle, James is the least familiar to us. The biblical account is practically devoid of any explicit details about his life and character. He never appears as a stand-alone character in the Gospel accounts, but he is always paired with his younger and better-known brother, John. The only time he is mentioned by himself is in the Book of Acts, where his martyrdom is recorded.

James figures prominently in the close inner circle of three.

Read the following Scriptures. Draw a line matching the reference with the experience James shared with Peter and John.

Matthew 17:1-3	Stay with Jesus in Gethsemane
Mark 5:35-43	Jesus' transfiguration
Mark 13:1-4	Raising of Jairus's daughter
Mark 14:32-34	Question Jesus about future events

As a member of the small inner circle, James was privileged to witness Jesus' *power* in the raising of the dead, he saw His *glory* when Jesus was transfigured, he saw Christ's *sovereignty* in the way the Lord unfolded the future to them on the Mount of Olives, and he saw the Savior's *agony* in the garden. All of these events must have strengthened his faith immensely and equipped him for the suffering and martyrdom he himself would eventually face.

If there's a key word that applies to the life of the Apostle James, that word is *passion*. From the little we know about him, it is obvious that he was a man of intense fervor and intensity. In fact, Jesus gave James and John a nickname: *Boanerges*—"Sons of Thunder." That defines James's

Week of AUGUST 7

personality in very vivid terms. He was zealous, thunderous, passionate, and fervent.

There is a legitimate place in spiritual leadership for people who have thunderous personalities. Elijah was that kind of character. (Indeed, Elijah was the role model James thought he was following when he pleaded for fire from heaven.) Nehemiah was similarly passionate (see Nehemiah 13:25). John the Baptist had a fiery temperament too. James apparently was cut from similar fabric. He was outspoken, intense, and impatient with evildoers.

Whenever zeal disintegrates into uncontrolled passion, it can be deadly. And James sometimes had a tendency to let such misguided zeal get the better of him. Two incidents in particular illustrate this. One is the episode where James wanted to call down fire. The other is the time James and John enlisted their mother's help to lobby for the highest seats in the kingdom. Let's look at these incidents over the next two days.

Fire from Heaven

We get our best glimpse of why James and John were known as the Sons of Thunder in Luke 9:51–56. Read it in the margin. It was significant that Jesus chose to travel through Samaria. The Jews regarded the Samaritans as a mongrel race and their religion as a mongrel religion. And the Samaritans hated the Jews and their worship as much as the Jews hated them and their worship. Along the way, Jesus and His followers would need places to eat and spend the night. Jesus sent messengers ahead to arrange accommodations. The Samaritans refused Jesus' messengers accommodations. The Samaritans were being deliberately inhospitable.

James and John, the Sons of Thunder, were instantly filled with passionate outrage.

In the Scripture in the margin, underline the remedy James and John had in mind for this situation.

"Now it came to pass, when the time had come for Him to be received up, that He steadfastly set His face to go to Jerusalem, and sent messengers before His face. And as they went, they entered a village of the Samaritans, to prepare for Him. But they did not receive Him, because His face was set for the journey to Jerusalem. And when His disciples James and John saw this, they said, 'Lord, do You want us to command fire to come down from heaven and consume them, just as Elijah did?' But He turned and rebuked them, and said, 'You do not know what manner of spirit you are of. For the Son of Man did not come to destroy men's lives but to save them.' And they went to another village" (Luke 9:51-56, NKJV).

The reference to Elijah was full of significance. The story of Elijah's fiery triumph to which James and John were referring had taken place in this very region (see 2 Kings 1). They were familiar with the Old Testament account, and they knew its historical relevance to Samaria. So when James and John suggested fire from heaven as a fitting response to the Samaritans' inhospitality, they probably thought they were standing on solid precedent. After all, Elijah was not condemned for his actions. On the contrary, at that time and under those circumstances, it was the appropriate response from Elijah.

But it was not a proper response for James and John. In the first place, their motives were wrong.

In the Scripture in the margin on page 117, circle the one word in James's and John's question that indicate a tone of arrogance.

Did you circle the word "us"? Of course, they did not have the power to call down fire from heaven. Christ was the only one in their company who had such power. If that were an appropriate response, He could well have done it Himself.

Furthermore, Jesus' mission was very different from Elijah's.

Once again read the Scripture in the margin on page 117. Fill in the blanks to state Jesus' mission.

Jesus came to s_____ men, not d_____ them.

Jesus' example taught James that loving-kindness and mercy are virtues to be cultivated as much as (and sometimes more than) righteous indignation and fiery zeal. Notice what happened. Instead of calling down fire from heaven, "They went to another village" (Luke 9:56). They simply found accommodations elsewhere. It was a little inconvenient, perhaps, but far better and far more appropriate in those circumstances than James's and John's proposed remedy for the Samaritans' inhospitality.

Week of AUGUST 7

Thrones in the Kingdom

Read Matthew 20:20-24 in your Bible. Circle character qualities displayed by James.

Humility   **Insensitivity**   **Apathy**

Overconfidence   **Passion**   **Ambition**

James and his brother John engaged in a furtive attempt to gain status over the other apostles. By comparing Matthew 27:56 with Mark 16:1, we further discover that the mother of James and John was named Salome. She was one of "many women who followed Jesus from Galilee, ministering to Him" (Matthew 27:55)—meaning that they supplied financial support and probably helped prepare meals (see Luke 8:1–3).

The idea for Salome's bold request was undoubtedly hatched in the minds of James and John because of Jesus' promise in Matthew 19:28. The promise of thrones caught the attention of James and John. So they decided to have their mother request that they be given the most prominent thrones.

James and John's ambition ultimately created conflicts among the apostles, because the other ten heard about it and were displeased. The question of who deserved the most prominent thrones became the big debate among them, and they carried it right to the table at the last supper (Luke 22:24).

Jesus' reply subtly reminded them that suffering is the prelude to glory (Matthew 20:22–23). James wanted a crown of glory; Jesus gave him a cup of suffering. He wanted power; Jesus gave him servanthood. He wanted a place of prominence; Jesus gave him a martyr's grave. He wanted to rule; Jesus gave him a sword—not to wield, but to be the instrument of his own execution. Fourteen years after this, James would become the first of the Twelve to be killed for his faith.

> "Jesus said to them, 'I assure you: In the Messianic Age, when the Son of Man sits on His glorious throne, you who have followed Me will also sit on 12 thrones, judging the 12 tribes of Israel'" (Matthew 19:28, HCSB).

A Cup of Suffering

The end of James's story from an earthly perspective is recorded in Acts 12:1–3. This is the one place in Scripture where James appears alone.

Read Acts 12:1-3 in your Bible. State the details of James's death.

_____

James is the only apostle whose death is actually recorded in Scripture.

That Son of Thunder had been mentored by Christ, empowered by the Holy Spirit, and shaped by those means into a man whose zeal and ambition were useful instruments in the hands of God for spreading of the kingdom. Still courageous, zealous, and committed to the truth, he had apparently learned to use those qualities for the Lord's service rather than for his own self-aggrandizement. And now his strength was so great that when Herod decided it was time to stop the church, James was the first man who had to die. He thus drank the cup Christ gave him to drink.

James is the prototype of the passionate, zealous, front runner who is dynamic, strong, and ambitious. Ultimately, his passions were tempered by sensitivity and grace. Somewhere along the line he had learned to control his anger, bridle his tongue, redirect his zeal, eliminate his thirst for revenge, and completely lose his selfish ambition. And the Lord used him to do a wonderful work in the early church.

How have you allowed the Lord to redirect your passions?

_____

_____

How has your exploration into James's life:

Encouraged you? _____

_____

Challenged you? _____

_____

Week of AUGUST 7

John—The Apostle of Love

The Apostle John is familiar to us because he wrote so much of the New Testament. He was the human author of a Gospel and three epistles that bear his name, as well as the Book of Revelation. Most of what we know about John we extract from his own writings.

John was the younger brother of James, and although he was a frequent companion to Peter in the first twelve chapters of Acts, Peter remained in the foreground and John remained in the background. But John also had his turn at leadership. Because he outlived all the others, he filled a unique and patriarchal role in the early church that lasted nearly to the end of the first century and reached deep into Asia Minor. His personal influence was indelibly stamped on the primitive church, well into the post-apostolic era.

Almost everything we observed about the personality and character of James is also true of John, the younger half of the Boanerges Brothers duo. The two men had similar temperaments and were inseparable in the Gospel accounts. Therefore it is all the more remarkable that John has often been nicknamed "the apostle of love."

Love was a quality John *learned* from Christ, not something that came naturally to him. In his younger years, he was as much a Son of Thunder as James. If you imagine that John was the way he was often portrayed in medieval art—a meek, mild, pale-skinned, effeminate person, lying around on Jesus' shoulder looking up at Him with a dove-eyed stare—forget that caricature. He was rugged and hard-edged, just like the rest of the fishermen-disciples. And again, he was every bit as intolerant, ambitious, zealous, and explosive as his elder brother. In fact, the one and only time the synoptic Gospel writers recorded John speaking for himself, he displayed his trademark aggressive, self-assertive, impertinent intolerance. So it is clear from the Gospel accounts that John was capable of behaving in the most sectarian, narrow-minded, unbending, reckless, and impetuous fashion. He was volatile. He was brash. He was aggressive. He was passionate, zealous, and personally ambitious—just like his brother James.

> "Under the control of the Holy Spirit, all [John's] liabilities were exchanged for assets."
> —John MacArthur

This was true for all of the apostles. How has it been true in your life?

_____

_____

But John aged well. Under the control of the Holy Spirit, all his liabilities were exchanged for assets. Compare the young disciple with the aged patriarch, and you'll see that as he matured, his areas of greatest weakness all developed into his greatest strengths. He's an amazing example of what should happen to us as we grow in Christ—allowing the Lord's strength to be made perfect in our weakness.

HE LEARNED THE BALANCE OF LOVE AND TRUTH

Love did not nullify the Apostle John's passion for truth. Rather, it gave him the balance he needed. John's love of truth is evident in all his writings. He uses the Greek word for *truth* twenty-five times in his Gospel and twenty more times in his epistles. No one in all of Scripture, except the Lord Himself, had more to say extolling the very concept of truth.

But sometimes in his younger years, John's zeal for truth was lacking in love and compassion for people. He needed to learn the balance.

Read Mark 9:38-41 in your Bible. Why did John tell the man to stop casting out demons in Jesus' name?

_____

What does this tell you about John's character?

_____

This is the one place in the synoptic Gospels where John acts and speaks alone, so it is an important insight into his character. Here we see clearly that John was not a passive personality. He was aggressive. He was competitive. He condemned a man who was ministering in the name of Jesus, just because the man wasn't part of their group. John had actually stepped in and tried to shut down this man's ministry for no other reason than that.

I believe this was a major turning point in John's life and thinking. He felt the sting of Jesus' rebuke. Something in John was beginning to change, and he was beginning to see his own lack of love as undesirable. John had always been zealous and passionate for the truth, but now the Lord was teaching him to love.

Many people place too much emphasis on the love side of the fulcrum. Some are merely ignorant about what is true; others are deceived; still others simply do not care about what is true. In each case, truth is

Week of AUGUST 7

missing, and all they are left with is error, clothed in a shallow, tolerant sentimentality. They talk a lot about love and tolerance, but they utterly lack any concern for the truth.

On the other hand, there are many who have all their theological ducks in a row and know their doctrine but are unloving and self-exalting. They are left with truth as cold facts, stifling and unattractive. Their lack of love cripples the power of the truth they profess to revere.

The truly godly person must cultivate both virtues in equal proportions. Pursue a perfect balance of truth and love. Know the truth, and uphold it in love. Truth is never to be abandoned in the name of love. But love is not to be deposed in the name of truth.

We noted that John used the word *truth* some forty-five times in his Gospel and epistles. But it is interesting that he also used the word *love* more than eighty times. Clearly, he learned the balance Christ taught Him. He learned to love others as the Lord had loved him. Love became the anchor and centerpiece of the truth he was most concerned with.

Where do you lie in the balance between Love and Truth? Mark your response on the line below.

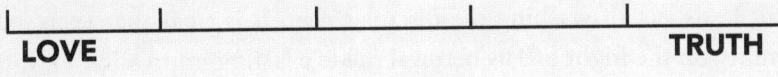
LOVE   **TRUTH**

How can you move toward a godly balance?
_____

More Balances Learned

HE LEARNED THE BALANCE OF AMBITION AND HUMILITY

In his youth, John had some ambitious plans for himself. In Mark 10, one chapter after the incident where John rebuked a man who was ministering in Jesus' name, we find Mark's description of how James and John approached Jesus with their request to be seated on His right and left in the kingdom. Coming as it did on the heels of so many admonitions from Jesus about humility, the brothers' request shows amazing audacity. It reveals how utterly devoid of true humility they were. Their ambition was untempered by humility. And Jesus had repeatedly made clear that the highest positions in the kingdom are reserved for the most humble saints on earth.

Read Jesus' response to James and John in Mark 10:42-45. Summarize the truth of Jesus' comments in one sentence.

John *did* eventually learn the balance between ambition and humility. In fact, humility is one of the great virtues that comes through in his writings. Throughout John's Gospel, for instance, he never once mentions his own name. (The only "John" who is mentioned by name in the Gospel of John is John the Baptist.) The Apostle John refuses to speak of himself in reference to himself. In fact, it is John's Gospel alone that records in detail Jesus' act of washing the disciples' feet. It is clear that Jesus' own humility on the night of His betrayal made a lasting impression on John.

HE LEARNED THE BALANCE OF SUFFERING AND GLORY

All the disciples wanted the chief seats in glory. But Jesus said there is a price for those seats. Not only are those seats reserved for the humble, but those who sit in those seats will first be prepared for the place of honor by enduring the humility of suffering. That is why Jesus told James and John that before they would receive any throne at all, they would be required to "drink the cup that I drink, and be baptized with the baptism that I am baptized with" (Mark 10:38). How eagerly and how naively James and John assured the Lord that they would be able to drink of the cup He would drink and be baptized with a baptism of suffering (v. 39).

When John's brother James became the church's first martyr, John bore the loss in a more personal way than the others. As each of the other disciples was martyred one by one, John suffered the grief and pain of additional loss. These were his friends and companions. Soon he alone was left. In some ways, that may have been the most painful suffering

Week of AUGUST 7

of all. John was the only disciple who lived to old age. He suffered in ways the others did not. He was still enduring earthly anguish and persecution long after the others were already in glory.

Virtually all reliable sources in early church history attest to the fact that John became the pastor of the church the Apostle Paul had founded at Ephesus. From there, during a great persecution of the church under the Roman Emperor Domitian (brother and successor of Titus, who destroyed Jerusalem), John was banished to a prison community on Patmos, one of the small Dodecanese Islands in the Aegean Sea off the west coast of modern Turkey. He lived in a cave there. It was while there that he received and recorded the apocalyptic visions described in the Book of Revelation. It was a harsh environment for an aged man. He was cut off from those whom he loved, treated with cruelty and reproach, and made to sleep on a stone slab with a rock for a pillow as the years passed slowly. John died, by most accounts, around A.D. 98, during the reign of Emperor Trajan.

John learned the lessons. He became a choice human model of what righteous, Christlike character ought to be. Powerful proof of this is seen in a vignette from the cross. John is the only one of the apostles whom the biblical record places as an eyewitness to the crucifixion. John himself describes the scene as Jesus looked down from the cross and saw His mother and John (John 19:25). John writes, "When Jesus therefore saw His mother, and the disciple whom He loved standing by, He said to His mother, 'Woman, behold your son!' Then He said to the disciple, 'Behold your mother!' And from that hour that disciple took her to his own home" (vv. 26–27). John had learned to be a humble, loving servant—or else Jesus would not have given him the care of His own mother. Several witnesses in early church history record that John never left Jerusalem and never left the care of Mary until she died.

As you ponder the life of the Apostle John, what has

Encouraged you? _____

_____

Challenged you? _____

_____

NOTES

To the Leader:

Read 2 John 1 and 3 John 1. Pray for the courage and wisdom to balance love and truth as you lead adults to study God's Word and deepen their relationship with Christ.

Before the Session:

1. For Step 6, prepare this handout: Group One: Read 1 John 1:8-10; 2:4-6. How does John demonstrate a passion for truth? How is his passion for truth balanced by love? Group Two: Read 1 John 3:16-18; 4:19-21. How does John demonstrate a passion for love? How is that passion balanced by truth?

During the Session:

1. Invite volunteers to share what words come to mind when they hear the word *thunder.* Comment that these terms can be used to describe the apostles James and John, nicknamed the "Sons of Thunder" by Jesus.   OR   Invite volunteers to share crazy things they and their siblings did growing up. Ask: *Were you the kind of siblings the relatives and neighbors cringed to see coming? Why? What do you think the people of Capernaum felt about two brothers called the "Sons of Thunder?" Why?* Explain that "Sons of Thunder" was Jesus' nickname for the apostles James and John.   FOR BOTH OPTIONS   Comment you will look at Scriptures today that demonstrate the brothers' thunderous personalities and show how their relationship with the Lord tempered their thunder into a positive rather than a negative force. This study will challenge learners to let God transform their zeal and passions.

2. Ask a volunteer to read Luke 9:51-56 from the margin of Day 2. Ask how the brothers' thunderous personalities are evident in this passage. Ask if that type of personality is ever appropriate in God's kingdom and why. To explore the appropriate time and place for passionate zeal, organize the class into two groups. Instruct one group to complete the activity about Nehemiah in the margin of Day 1. Direct the second group to read 2 Kings 1:2-17 and apply the questions in the margin of Day 1 to the passage about Elijah. Allow groups to share what they discussed. Explore why James's and John's passionate response in Luke 9 was inappropriate and what the brothers learned from this experience. Use the comments in Day 2 to add to your discussion.

Week of AUGUST 7

3. Invite someone to read Matthew 20:20-23. Ask what else James and John were passionate about. [themselves, power] Ask: *Do you think this was Salome's idea or did her boys put her up to it? Explain.* (If most learners have children, you may want to spend some time discussing what parents can learn from this passage. Encourage parents to seek God's best, not the world's best, for their children.) Request learners silently read Matthew 20:24-28 to discover the responses of the other apostles and of Jesus to the brothers' request. (Or, you can discuss the first activity in Day 5, which refers to a parallel passage to Matthew 20.)
4. Request someone read Acts 12:1-3. Ask: *What was James passionate about at the end of his life? How was passion for himself transformed into passion for Jesus?* Refer learners to the first activity and comments in Day 1 for help in answering this question. Ask why learners think James was the first of the faithful apostles to die. Discuss the last activity of Day 3.
5. Comment that in contrast to James, who died first for Christ, his brother John was the last apostle to die. Request someone read John 19:25-27 and ask if learners can find a reason for John's death coming so much later. [He was taking care of Jesus' mother, Mary.] Remark that we don't all have to demonstrate devotion to Jesus in the same way—the main way we show Jesus we love Him is by being obedient to what He asks us to do.
6. Read the quotation by John MacArthur in the margin of Day 4. Request learners search Day 4 and name some of John's liabilities. Ask a volunteer to read Mark 9:38-41. Discuss the first activity in Day 4. Inquire: *John had a passion for truth. How can zeal for truth be damaging if it's exercised in your own strength? How does love balance truth?* Request that the class reorganize into the two groups they had formed earlier. Distribute the prepared handouts. Give groups time to discuss and then share their findings with the entire class.
7. Read aloud Revelation 1:9 and comment that John never lost his passion for Christ's love and truth. Discuss the last activity of Day 5.
8. Close in prayer, asking that learners allow Christ to transform their liabilities and weaknesses into His assets and strength.

NOTES

The Bean Counter and the Guileless One

Meet Philip

In the four biblical lists of the twelve apostles, the fifth name on every list is Philip. *Philip* is a Greek name meaning "lover of horses." He must also have had a Jewish name, because all twelve apostles were Jewish. But his Jewish name is never given. (Don't confuse him with Philip the deacon, the man we meet in Acts 6 who became an evangelist and led the Ethiopian eunuch to Christ.) The Apostle Philip "was from Bethsaida, the city of Andrew and Peter" (John 1:44). Philip probably grew up attending the same synagogue as Peter and Andrew. Because of the relationship that existed between Peter and Andrew and the sons of Zebedee, Philip was possibly acquainted with all four.

What do we know about Philip? All the vignettes of Philip appear in the Gospel of John. In John's narrative, Philip is often paired with Nathanael (also known as Bartholomew), so we can assume the two of them were close comrades.

PHILIP'S CALL

We first meet Philip in John 1:43, the day after Jesus had first called Andrew, John, and Peter. Apparently Philip was also in the wilderness with John the Baptist, and before returning to Galilee, Jesus sought him out and invited him to join the other disciples. This is the first time we read that Jesus Himself actually sought and found one of them. In the descriptions of how they first encountered Christ, this language is unique to the call of Philip. He is the first one whom Jesus physically sought out, and the first one to whom Jesus actually said, "Follow Me."

Week of AUGUST 14

But Philip already had a seeking heart. Philip's seeking heart is evident in how he responded to Jesus. "Philip found Nathanael and said to him, 'We have found Him of whom Moses in the law, and also the prophets, wrote; Jesus of Nazareth, the son of Joseph'" (John 1:45). Obviously, Philip and Nathanael, like the first four disciples, had been studying the Law and the Prophets and were seeking the Messiah. That is why they had all gone to the wilderness to hear John the Baptist.

Philip not only had a seeking heart, but he also had the heart of a personal evangelist.

Read John 1:43-45 in your Bible. What is the first thing Philip did after meeting Jesus?

found Nathanael + said "we have found Him...."

Do you remember what the first thing you did after meeting Jesus was?

I am convinced that friendships provide the most fertile soil for evangelism. And it seems that invariably, when someone becomes a true follower of Christ, that person's first impulse is to want to find a friend and introduce that friend to Christ. That dynamic is seen in Philip's spontaneous instinct to go find Nathanael and tell him about the Messiah.

The language Philip used betrayed his amazement at discovering who the Messiah was. The One of whom Moses wrote, and the One foretold by the prophets, was none other than "Jesus of Nazareth, the son of Joseph," a lowly carpenter's son.

Philip knew the Old Testament promises. He was ready. He was expectant. His heart was prepared. And he received Jesus gladly, unhesitatingly, as Messiah. No reluctance. No disbelief. It mattered not to him what kind of one-horse town the Messiah had grown up in. Philip knew instantly that he had come to the end of his search.

day Two

Feeding of the Five Thousand

How might a person with Philip's natural administrative personality respond to each of the situations below?

After his experience on the mountainside that day, how would Philip have advised you to respond to each situation?

1. Your teenager expresses a strong calling to go on a costly overseas mission trip.

_____

2. Your church leadership has expressed the need for an additional full-time staff member and/or additional educational space.

_____

3. Your spouse feels led to make a sacrificial gift to the Lottie Moon Christmas Offering for International Missions.

_____

Our next glimpse of Philip occurs in John 6, at the feeding of the five thousand. Here we discover what Philip as a natural man was like. Here his natural personality begins to show through. John describes how a great multitude had sought out Jesus and found Him on a mountainside with His disciples. To say this was a crowd of five thousand doesn't do justice to the size of the multitude. John 6:10 says there were five thousand *men* in the crowd. There must have been several more thousand women and children. According to Matthew 14:15, evening was approaching. The people needed to eat. John 6:5 says, "Then Jesus lifted up His eyes, and seeing a great multitude coming toward Him, He said to Philip, 'Where shall we buy bread, that these may eat?'"

Why did Jesus single Philip out and ask him? John says, "This He said to test him, for He Himself knew what He would do" (v. 6). Philip was apparently the apostolic administrator—the bean counter. It is likely that he was charged with arranging meals and logistics. We know that Judas was in charge of keeping the money (John 13:29), so it makes sense that someone was also charged with coordinating the acquisition and distribution of meals and supplies.

So Jesus was testing Philip. He wasn't testing him to find out what he was thinking; Jesus already knew that (see John 2:25). He wasn't asking for a plan; John says Jesus also already knew what He Himself was going to do. He was testing Philip so that Philip would reveal to himself what he was like. That is why Jesus turned to Philip, the classic administrative personality, and asked, "How do you propose to feed all these people?"

I believe Philip had already begun counting heads. When the crowd started moving in, he was already doing estimates. It was late in the day; this was a huge crowd; they were going to be hungry. There were no fast-food franchises on that mountainside. So by the time Jesus asked the question, Philip already had his calculations prepared: "Philip answered Him, 'Two hundred denarii worth of bread is not sufficient for them, that

Week of AUGUST 14

every one of them may have a little'" (John 6:7). Instead of thinking, *What a glorious occasion! Jesus is going to teach this crowd. What a tremendous opportunity for the Lord!*—all pessimistic Philip could see was the impossibility of the situation.

Philip had been there when the Lord created wine out of water (John 2:2). But when he saw that great crowd, he began to feel overwhelmed by the impossible. He lapsed into materialistic thinking. And when Jesus tested his faith, he responded with open unbelief. *It can't be done.* He had already figured out that four thousand barley cakes would never be enough to go around. His thoughts were pessimistic, analytical, and pragmatic—completely materialistic and earthbound.

Philip was obsessed with mundane matters and therefore overwhelmed by the impossibility of the immediate problem. He knew too much arithmetic to be adventurous. The reality of the raw facts clouded his faith. He was so obsessed with this temporal predicament that he was oblivious to the transcendental possibilities that lay in Jesus' power. He was so enthralled with common-sense calculations that he didn't see the opportunity the situation presented. He *should* have said, "Lord, if You want to feed them, feed them. I'm just going to stand back and watch how You do it. I know You can do it, Lord. You made wine at Cana and fed Your children manna in the wilderness. Do it. We will tell everyone to get in line, and You just make the food." That would have been the right response. But Philip was convinced it simply couldn't be done. The limitless supernatural power of Christ had completely escaped his thinking.

What personal experience threatens to overwhelm you? _new job_

What seems impossible about this situation? _∅ experience_

What does Philip's experience in John 6 challenge you to do about this situation? _____

The Visit of the Greeks

John 12 gives us another insight into Philip's character. Again we see his overanalytical temperament. He was concerned too much about methods and protocol. He lacked boldness and vision. It made him too timid and too apprehensive. And when he had another opportunity to step out in faith, he missed it again.

Read John 12:20–21 about the Greeks who came to Philip asking to see Jesus. These were either God-fearing Gentiles or full-fledged proselytes to Judaism who were coming to Jerusalem to worship God at the Passover. This was the final Passover of the Old Testament economy, during which Jesus Himself would be slain as the true Lamb of God.

These Greeks were very interested in Jesus. They sought out Philip in particular. Perhaps because of his Greek name, they thought he was the best contact. Again we see that Philip seems to have been the one in charge of operations. So these men approached him to arrange a meeting with Jesus. It was not a difficult or complex request. And yet Philip seems to have been unsure what to do with them. Nonetheless, Philip took the Greeks to Andrew. Andrew would bring anyone to Jesus (John 12:22).

The Upper Room

Our final glimpse of Philip comes just a short time later, in the Upper Room with the disciples on the occasion of the last supper. It is significant to note that this was the last night of Jesus' earthly ministry—the eve of His crucifixion.

Jesus announced He was going away (John 14:1–3). Then He added an explicit claim about His own deity: "If you had known Me, you would have known My Father also; and from now on you know Him and have seen Him" (John 14:7). Jesus was stating in the clearest possible language that He is God. Christ and His Father are of the same essence. To know Christ is to know the Father.

Week of AUGUST 14

Read John 14:8 in your Bible. Indicate how you feel about Philip's response to Jesus. (Check one and complete the statement.)

I think it's a legitimate request because _____

I think it's sad because _he was in the presence of God himself._

Other: _____

"Jesus said to him, 'Have I been with you so long, and yet you have not known Me, Philip? He who has seen Me has seen the Father; so how can you say, "Show us the Father"?'" (v. 9). What did Philip think had been going on for the past two or three years? How could Philip of all people, who had responded with such enthusiastic faith at the beginning, be making a request like this at the end? Where was his faith? Then Jesus asked him, "Do you not believe that I am in the Father, and the Father in Me? The words that I speak to you I do not speak on My own authority; but the Father who dwells in Me does the works. Believe Me that I am in the Father and the Father in Me, or else believe Me for the sake of the works themselves" (vv. 10–11).

Notice the appeal: "Do you not believe? . . . *Believe*"! Philip had already embraced Jesus as Messiah. Christ was urging him to take his faith to its logical conclusion: Philip was already in the presence of the living and eternal God Himself. For three years Philip had gazed into the very face of God, and it still was not clear to him. His earthbound thinking, his skepticism, his obsession with mundane details, his preoccupation with business details, and his small-mindedness had shut him off from a full apprehension of whose presence he had enjoyed. He was slow to understand, slow to trust, and slow to see beyond the immediate circumstances.

But tradition tells us that Philip was greatly used in the spread of the early church and was among the first of the apostles to suffer martyrdom. By most accounts he was put to death by stoning at Heliopolis, in Phrygia (Asia Minor), eight years after the martyrdom of James. Before Philip's death, multitudes came to Christ under his preaching.

Read John 14:10 in your Bible. When has Jesus had to ask you this question about your belief in Him?

_____

What was your answer?

_____

How did your study of Philip:

Encourage you? _Though Philip was narrow-minded & obsessed c earthly issues & details, he was greatly used by God._

Challenge you? _Move out in faith; don't get caught up in the "issue of the day."_

Nathanael—The Guileless One

Philip's closest companion, Nathanael, is listed as Bartholomew in all four lists of the Twelve. In the Gospel of John he is always called Nathanael. *Bartholomew* is a Hebrew surname meaning "son of Tolmai." *Nathanael* means "God has given." So he is Nathanael, son of Tolmai, or Nathanael Bar-Tolmai. The synoptic Gospels and the Book of Acts contain no details about Nathanael's background, character, or personality. In fact, they each mention him only once—when they list all twelve disciples. John's Gospel features Nathanael in just two passages: in John 1, where his call is recorded, and in John 21:2, where he is named as one of those who returned to Galilee and went fishing with Peter after Jesus' resurrection and before the ascension.

According to John 21:2, Nathanael came from the small town of Cana in Galilee, the place where Jesus did His first miracle, changing water into wine (John 2:11). Cana was very close to Jesus' own hometown, Nazareth. As we saw above, Nathanael was brought to Jesus by Philip immediately after Philip was sought and called by Christ. Philip and Nathanael were apparently close friends, because in each of the synoptic Gospels' lists of the twelve apostles, the names of Philip and Bartholomew are linked.

Virtually everything we know about Nathanael Bar-Tolmai comes from John's account of his call to discipleship. Remember, that event took place in the wilderness, shortly after Jesus' baptism, when John the Baptist pointed to Christ as the Lamb of God who takes away the sin of the world (John 1:29). According to verse 45, "Philip found Nathanael." They were obviously friends. Whether this was a business relationship, a family relationship, or just a social relationship, Scripture does not say. But Philip obviously was close to Nathanael, and he knew Nathanael would be interested in the news that the long-awaited Messiah had finally been identified. So he immediately pursued him and brought him to Jesus.

The brief description of how Nathanael came to Jesus is full of insight into his character. We learn quite a lot about what kind of person he was.

Week of AUGUST 14

HIS LOVE OF SCRIPTURE

One striking fact about Nathanael is obvious from how Philip announced to him that he had found the Messiah. Philip didn't say to Nathanael, "I found a man who has a wonderful plan for your life." He didn't say, "I found a man who will fix your marriage and your personal problems and give your life meaning." He didn't appeal to Nathanael on the basis of how Jesus might make *Nathanael's* life better. Rather, "Philip found Nathanael and said to him, 'We have found Him of whom Moses in the law, and also the prophets, wrote'" (John 1:45). Obviously, the truth of Scripture was something that mattered to Nathanael. Therefore, when Philip told Nathanael about the Messiah, he did so from the standpoint of Old Testament prophecy. The fact that Philip introduced Jesus this way suggests that Nathanael *knew* the Old Testament prophecies. Nathanael had been such a diligent student of Scripture.

HIS PREJUDICE

Read John 1:46 in your Bible. What insight do you gain into Nathanael's character?
❑ **He was compassionate.**
☑ **He was prejudiced.**
❑ **He was politically correct.**

Nathanael might have said, "As I read the Old Testament, Micah the prophet says Messiah comes out of Bethlehem [Micah 5:2], not Nazareth." But the depth of his prejudice comes through in the words he chose: "Can anything good come out of Nazareth?" That was not a rational or biblical objection; it was based on sheer emotion and bigotry. It reveals what contempt Nathanael had for the whole town of Nazareth.

Nazareth was a rough town. Its culture was largely unrefined and uneducated. The Judaeans looked down on all Galileans, but even the Galileans looked down on the Nazarenes. Nathanael, though he came from an even more lowly village, was simply echoing the Galileans' general contempt for Nazareth. It was inconceivable to Nathanael that the Messiah would come out of a tacky place like Nazareth.

Prejudice is ugly. Generalizations based on feelings of superiority, not on fact, can be spiritually debilitating. Prejudice cuts a lot of people off from the truth.

What steps might you take to "come and see" a person or group of people against whom you harbor prejudice?

_____

Fortunately, Nathanael's prejudice wasn't strong enough to keep him from Christ. "Philip said to him, 'Come and see'" (v. 46). That is the right way to deal with prejudice: Confront it with the facts. Prejudice is feeling-based. It is subjective. It does not necessarily reflect the reality of the matter. So the remedy for prejudice is an honest look at objective reality—"come and see."

And Nathanael went. Fortunately, his prejudiced mind was not as powerful as his seeking heart.

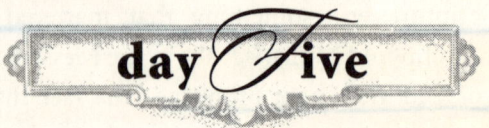

A True Israelite

His Sincerity of Heart

The most important aspect of Nathanael's character is expressed from the lips of Jesus. Jesus knew Nathanael already. Jesus saw Nathanael coming toward Him and said of him, "Behold, an Israelite indeed, in whom is no deceit!" (John 1:47).

Can you imagine a more wonderful thing than to have words of approval like that come out of the mouth of Jesus? This speaks volumes about Nathanael's character. He was pure-hearted from the beginning. Certainly he was human. He had sinful faults. His mind was tainted by a degree of prejudice. But His heart was not poisoned by deceit. He was no hypocrite. His love for God and His desire to see the Messiah were genuine. His heart was sincere and without guile. Jesus refers to him as "an Israelite indeed." The word in the Greek text is *alethos,* meaning "truly, genuinely." He was an authentic Israelite. This is not a reference to his physical descent from Abraham. Jesus was linking Nathanael's status as a true Israelite to the fact that he was without deceit. His guilelessness is what defined him as a true Israelite.

This is very unusual, and it was particularly rare in first-century Israel. Remember, Jesus indicted the entire religious establishment of His day as hypocrites. But here was a true, nonhypocritical Jew. Here was a man whose heart was circumcised, cleansed of defilement. His faith was

Week of AUGUST 14

authentic. His devotion to God was real. He was without guile, not like the scribes and Pharisees. He was a truly righteous man—flawed by sin as we all are—but justified before God through a true and living faith.

His Eager Faith

Jesus seemed to know everything about Nathanael. "Nathanael said to Him, 'How do You know me?'" (John 1:48). "Jesus answered and said to him, 'Before Philip called you, when you were under the fig tree, I saw you'" (v. 48). This put a whole different spin on things. This was not flattery; it was omniscience! Jesus wasn't physically present to see Nathanael under the fig tree; Nathanael knew that. Suddenly he realized he was standing in the presence of someone who could see into his very heart with an omniscient eye.

What was the significance of the fig tree? It was most likely the place where Nathanael went to study and meditate on Scripture. In effect, Jesus was saying, "I know the state of your heart because I saw you under the fig tree. I knew what you were doing. That was your private chamber. That's where you go to study and pray. That's where you go to meditate. And I saw you in that secret place. I knew what you were doing." It was not only that Jesus saw his *location,* but that He saw his *heart* as well. He knew the sincerity of Nathanael's character because He saw right into him when he was under the fig tree. That was enough for Nathanael. He "answered and said to Him, 'Rabbi, You are the Son of God! You are the King of Israel!'" (v. 49).

Jesus affirmed Nathanael's faith and promised that he would see even greater things than a simple show of Jesus' omniscience. That's all we know about Nathanael from Scripture. Early church records suggest that he ministered in Persia and India and took the gospel as far as Armenia. There is no reliable record of how he died. One tradition says he was tied up in a sack and cast into the sea. Another tradition says he was crucified. By all accounts he was martyred.

How did a brief look into Nathanael's life:

Encourage you? _____

_____

Challenge you? *push beyond prejudice*

_____

If you desire to dig deeper...

Read Matthew 6:5-8 in your Bible.

Why do you think Jesus was so impressed with Nathanael's prayer life?

_____

What would Jesus say about your private life with Him?

_____

NOTES

To the Leader:

You have noticed in your study of the apostles so far that no two men were alike, yet they were all valuable to Jesus. The learners in your class are not alike either—they have different needs, personalities, and learning styles. Be willing to move beyond your comfort zone and try a new teaching method. It might not be the style that best fits you or the majority of your class, but it might be exactly what one person in your class needs. Try it!

During the Session

1. Ask: *Have you had a friend who was your total opposite? Describe that friendship. How did your differences cause friction at times? How did your differences complement one another and make you both better people?* Comment that Philip and Nathanael appear to have been close friends with very different personalities. Yet Jesus chose both of them to be His apostles. Learners can learn how to be more committed to Christ through studying Philip's and Nathanael's strengths and weaknesses. OR Ask, *How would you respond if our pastor asked you to be in charge of a banquet for 5,000 people?* Organize the class into several small groups and direct them to plan this banquet—outlining steps they would take in preparation and the food they would serve. Allow groups to share. Comment that this exercise might help learners identify with how Philip felt when the Lord asked how he proposed to feed a crowd of well over 5,000 people.

2. To examine Philip's initial call to follow Jesus, invite someone to read John 1:43. Ask: *How do we know Jesus really wanted Philip to be part of His small group of followers? Later on we'll discover Philip failed tests of faith—how do you think his original calling encouraged him to keep going? How does the fact that Jesus took the initiative to find and save you encourage you to keep striving to follow Him even after you have really messed up?* Discuss the activity in Day 1. Ask what impression learners have of Philip so far.

3. Comment that the next time Philip appears in Scripture he doesn't come across in such a good light. Request a volunteer to read John 6:1-13. Explain Philip's likely role as administrator for this band of men. Guide the class to state characteristics of Philip that are evident from his response in verse 7. (Search Day 2 for ideas.) Ask: *Do you think this biblical episode teaches there's not a place for administrative personalities in God's kingdom? What's the point of this interchange between Jesus and Philip?* Discuss the case studies in the margin of Day 2.

Week of AUGUST 14

4. Invite someone to read John 12:20-22. Inquire: *What's good in how Philip responded?* [At least he didn't turn them away!] *Why do you think he didn't take the men to Jesus himself? How do you think he felt afterward?* Invite volunteers to share times they missed an opportunity to lead someone to Jesus and how they felt about it. Be prepared to share from your own experience. Discuss how learners can turn a negative experience of failing to witness into something positive. [It makes you more dependent on Christ. It makes you more determined and prepared to not miss an opportunity the next time.]
5. Invite someone to read John 14:1-11. Discuss the first activity of Day 3. Ask the class to compare Philip's response in verse 8 to his initial response to Jesus in John 1:45. Ask how believers can move from excitement about Jesus to a blindness about who He really is. [Sample responses might be that persons lose faith when they try to make Jesus fit their idea of what a Savior should be or when they simply let life get in the way.] Acknowledge that it is not always pleasant to evaluate yourself in the light of someone else's failures. Allow volunteers to share their responses to the final activity of Day 3.
6. Request a volunteer read John 1:45-51. Guide the class to list details about Nathanael and insights into his character gained from reading this short passage. Use the information given in Days 4 and 5 to add to the discussion. Allow volunteers to share their responses to the final activity in Day 5.
7. Discuss the margin activity about prejudice from Day 4. Challenge learners to list specific steps they can take to actually get to know someone against whom they have been prejudiced. Discuss actions the class can take that will challenge learners to move beyond their prejudice against groups of people. [Examples: Host a baby shower for residents of a home for unwed mothers. Provide and serve a meal at a homeless shelter. Become involved in a local ministry to AIDS patients or jail inmates.]

NOTES

After the Session

Enlist learners to plan a class ministry project using ideas discussed during Step 7.

' # The Tax Collector and The Twin

Matthew the Publican

In all likelihood, none of the Twelve was more notorious as a sinner than Matthew. He is called by his Jewish name, "Levi the son of Alphaeus," in Mark 2:14. Luke refers to him as "Levi" in Luke 5:27–29 and as "Matthew" when he lists the Twelve in Luke 6:15 and Acts 1:13.

Matthew, of course, is the author of the Gospel that bears his name. For that reason, we might expect to have a lot of detail about this man and his character. But the fact of the matter is that we know very little about Matthew. He kept himself almost completely in the background throughout his lengthy account of Jesus' life and ministry. In his entire Gospel he mentions his own name only two times. Once is where he records his call, and the other is when he lists all twelve apostles.

Matthew was a tax collector—a publican—when Jesus called him. That is the *last* credential we might expect to see from a man who would become an apostle of Christ, a top leader in the church, and a preacher of the gospel. After all, tax collectors were the most despised people in Israel. They were hated and vilified by all of Jewish society. They were deemed lower than Herodians (Jews who were loyal to the Idumean dynasty of the Herods) and more worthy of scorn than the occupying Roman soldiers. Publicans were men who had bought tax franchises from the Roman emperor and then extorted money from the people of Israel to feed the Roman coffers and to pad their own pockets. They often strong-armed money out of people with the use of thugs. Most were despicable, vile, unprincipled scoundrels.

Matthew 9:9 records the call of this man. It comes out of nowhere, completely catching the reader by surprise: "As Jesus passed on from

Week of AUGUST 21

[Capernaum], He saw a man named Matthew sitting at the tax office. And He said to him, 'Follow Me.' So he arose and followed Him." That is the only glimpse of Matthew we have from his own Gospel.

Matthew goes on in the next few verses to say, "Now it happened, as Jesus sat at the table in the house, that behold, many tax collectors and sinners came and sat down with Him and His disciples" (Matthew 9:10). Luke 5 reveals that this was actually an enormous banquet that Matthew himself held at his own house in Jesus' honor. It seems Matthew invited a large number of his fellow tax collectors and various other kinds of scoundrels and social outcasts to meet Jesus.

Read Luke 5:29-32 in your Bible.

Why did Matthew invite tax gatherers and other lowlifes to his banquet? _____

How do you think Matthew and his associates felt about Jesus attending a banquet with them? _____

_____

Why? _____

How did the religious elite feel about Jesus' presence in Matthew's house? _____

As we saw in the case of Philip and Andrew, Matthew's first impulse after following Jesus was to bring his closest friends and introduce them to the Savior. He was so thrilled to have found the Messiah that he wanted to introduce Jesus to everyone he knew. So he held a large banquet in Jesus' honor and invited them all.

For a *Jewish* man like Matthew to be a tax collector made him a traitor to the nation, a social pariah, the rankest of the rank. He would also have been a religious outcast, forbidden to enter any synagogue. Jesus and the apostles, however, according to Matthew's own account, gladly came and ate with such people.

Luke records what happened on that occasion. Read about it in Luke 5:29–32. The people of the religious establishment were outraged and scandalized. They wasted no time voicing their criticism to the disciples.

But Jesus replied by saying sick people are the very ones who need a physician. He had not come to call the self-righteous but sinners to repentance. In other words, there was nothing He could do for the religious elite as long as they insisted on keeping up their pious, hypocritical veneer. But people like Matthew who were prepared to confess their sin could be forgiven and redeemed.

Are you more like (circle your answer):

Matthew & his friends   or   the religious establishment?

What is Jesus calling you to do about your response?

A Little Mokhes

There were two kinds of tax collectors, the *Gabbai* and the *Mokhes*. The Gabbai were general tax collectors. They collected property tax, income tax, and the poll tax. These taxes were set by official assessments, so there was not as much graft at this level. The Mokhes, however, collected a duty on imports and exports, goods for domestic trade, and virtually anything that was moved by road. They set tolls on roads and bridges, they taxed beasts of burden and axles on transport wagons, and they charged a tariff on parcels, letters, and whatever else they could find to tax. Their assessments were often arbitrary and capricious.

There were two kinds of Mokhes—the Great Mokhes and the Little Mokhes. A Great Mokhes stayed behind the scenes and hired others to collect taxes for him. (Zaccheus was apparently a Great Mokhes—a "chief tax collector"—Luke 19:2.) Matthew was evidently a Little Mokhes, because he manned a tax office where he dealt with people face to face (Matthew 9:9). He was the one the people saw and resented most. He was the worst of the worst. No self-respecting Jew in his right mind would ever

Week of AUGUST 21

choose to be a tax collector. He had effectively cut himself off not only from his own people but also from his God. After all, since he was banned from the synagogue and forbidden to sacrifice and worship in the temple, he was in essence worse off religiously than a Gentile.

Therefore it must have been a stunning reality to Matthew when Jesus chose him. It came out of the blue. By Matthew's own account, Jesus saw him sitting in the tax office and simply said, "Follow Me" (Matthew 9:9). Matthew instantly and without hesitation "arose and followed Him." He abandoned the tax office. He left his toll booth and walked away from his cursed profession forever.

What was in Matthew that caused him to drop everything and follow Christ at once?

The best answer we can deduce is that whatever Matthew's tortured soul may have experienced because of the profession he had chosen to be in, down deep inside he was a Jew who knew and loved the Old Testament. He was spiritually hungry. At some point in his life, most likely *after* he had chosen his despicable career, he was smitten with a gnawing spiritual hunger and became a true seeker. Of course, God was seeking and drawing *him,* and the draw was irresistible.

We know that Matthew knew the Old Testament very well, because his Gospel quotes the Old Testament ninety-nine times. That is more times than Mark, Luke, and John combined! Matthew obviously had extensive familiarity with the Old Testament. In fact, he quotes out of the Law, out of the Psalms, and out of the Prophets—every section of the Old Testament. So he had a good working knowledge of all the Scriptures that were available to him. He must have pursued his study of the Old Testament on his own, because he couldn't hear the Word of God explained in any synagogue. Apparently, in a quest to fill the spiritual void in his life, he had turned to the Scriptures.

He believed in the true God. And because he knew the record of God's revelation, he understood the promises of the Messiah. He must have also known about Jesus, because sitting on the crossroads in a tax booth, he would have heard information all the time. So when Jesus showed up and called him to follow Him, he had enough faith to drop everything and follow.

This is virtually all we know of Matthew: He knew the Old Testament, he believed in God, he looked for the Messiah, he dropped everything immediately when he met Jesus, and in the joy of his new-found relationship, he embraced the outcasts of his world and introduced them to Jesus. Matthew stands as a vivid reminder that the Lord often chooses the most despicable people of this world, redeems them, gives them new hearts, and uses them in remarkable ways.

Tradition says Matthew ministered to the Jews both in Israel and abroad for many years before being martyred for his faith. The earliest traditions indicate he was burned at the stake. Thus this man who walked away from a lucrative career without ever giving it a second thought remained willing to give his all for Christ to the very end.

What about Matthew's experience with Jesus:

Encouraged you? _____

_____

Challenged you? _____

_____

Thomas the Pessimist

Thomas is usually nicknamed "Doubting Thomas," but that may not be the most fitting label for him. He was a better man than the popular lore would indicate.

Thomas, according to John 11:16 (KJV), was also called "Didymus," which means "the twin." Apparently he had a twin brother or a twin sister, but his twin is never identified in Scriptures.

Thomas is mentioned only once each in the three synoptic Gospels. In each case, he is simply named with the other eleven apostles in a list. We learn everything we know about his character from John's Gospel.

Week of AUGUST 21

It probably is fair to say that Thomas was a somewhat negative person. He was a worrywart. He was a brooder. He tended to be anxious and angst-ridden. He was like Eeyore in Winnie the Pooh. He anticipated the worst all the time. Pessimism, rather than doubt, seems to have been his besetting sin. Yet despite his pessimism, some wonderfully redeeming elements of his character come through in John's account of him.

John's first mention of Thomas is found in John 11:16. It is a single verse, but it speaks volumes about Thomas's real character.

Read John 11:1-8 in your Bible.
Why did Jesus want to return to Judea? _____

_____

Why had Jesus left Judea earlier? _____

_____

Jesus went beyond the Jordan and stayed there (John 10:40). Here word was sent to Jesus that Lazarus of Bethany was sick (John 11:1-2). Jesus had formed a close and loving relationship with this family. But Bethany was on the outskirts of Jerusalem. This presented a quandary. If Jesus went that close to Jerusalem, He was walking into the very teeth of the worst kind of hostility. John 10:39 says the Jewish leaders were seeking to seize Him. They were already determined to kill Him. He had eluded their grasp once already, but if He returned to Bethany, they were certain to find out, and they would try again to seize Him.

After Jesus knew Lazarus had died, "He said to the disciples, 'Let us go to Judea again'" (John 11:7). The disciples thought this was crazy. They said, "Rabbi, lately the Jews sought to stone You, and are You going there again?" (v. 8). They frankly did not want to go back to Jerusalem. Then Jesus told them plainly that Lazarus was dead and He was going to wake him up (vv. 11–14). Then Jesus added, "Let us go to him" (v. 15).

Now they understood. Jesus *had* to go back. He was determined to do so. There would be no talking Him out of it. To them, it must have seemed like the worst possible disaster. They were floundering in fear. They were convinced that if Jesus returned to Bethany, He would be killed. But He had made up His mind.

It was at this point that Thomas spoke up. Here is where we meet him for the first time in all the Gospel records.

Read John 11:16 in your Bible. What character qualities did Thomas reveal in his response?

_____

Are you basically (circle one):

a pessimist

or

an optimist?

If you circled pessimist, does your pessimism lead you to:
- ❏ **Step out in courage?**
- ❏ **Shrink back in fear?**
- ❏ **It depends on the day?**

Now that is pessimistic—but it is a heroic pessimism. Thomas could see nothing but disaster ahead. He was convinced Jesus was heading straight for a stoning. But if that is what the Lord was determined to do, Thomas was grimly determined to go and die with Him. You have to admire his courage.

It is not easy to be a pessimist. It is a miserable way to live. An optimist might have said, "Let's go; everything will work out. The Lord knows what He is doing. We will be fine." But the pessimist says, "He's going to die, and we're going to die with Him." Thomas at least had the courage to be loyal, even in the face of his pessimism. It is much easier for an optimist to be loyal. He always expects the best. It is hard for a pessimist to be loyal, because he is convinced the worst is going to happen. Heroic pessimism is real courage.

Thomas obviously had a deep devotion to Christ that could not be dampened even by his own pessimism. He had no illusion that following Jesus would be easy. All he could see were the jaws of death opening to swallow him. But he followed Jesus with an undaunted courage. He was resolved to die if necessary with his Lord rather than forsake Him. He would rather die than be left behind and separated from Christ.

Thomas was an example of strength to the rest of the apostles. It appears they collectively followed his lead at this point and said, "OK, let's go and die"—because they _did_ go with Jesus to Bethany.

Where Are You Going?

Thomas's profound love for the Lord shows up again in John 14.

Read John 14:1-5 in your Bible & answer the following: In their present state, what do you think the apostles heard Jesus say?
- ❏ I'm coming back for you.
- ❏ I'm leaving.
- ❏ I'm preparing a place for you.

Week of **AUGUST 21**

What do you think was going on inside Thomas when he heard Jesus voice these words?

_____

Again we see his pessimism. In essence, he was saying, "You're leaving. We'll never get where you are going. We don't even know *how* to get there. How are we supposed to get there?"

Here is a man with deep love. He is a man whose relationship with Christ was so strong that he never wanted to be severed from Him. His heart was broken as he heard Jesus speak of leaving them. He was shattered. The thought of losing Christ paralyzed him. He had become so attached to Jesus in those years that he would have been glad to die with Christ, but he could not think of living without Him. You have to admire his devotion to Christ.

This announcement was overwhelming for Thomas. And his worst fears came to pass. Jesus died and he didn't.

Read John 14:1 in your Bible again. What message did Thomas miss? _____

Why is that message particularly hard for a person with a pessimistic nature? _____

How can obeying that command transform a pessimist into a godly optimist? _____

Have your worst fears ever been realized? Describe briefly.

_____

Compare Psalm 30:5 with John 16:20. What truth is expressed in both Scriptures?

_____

When did Thomas discover that truth?

_____

How have you discovered that truth?

_____

Seeing Is Believing

We pick up the next picture of Thomas in John 20. After Jesus' death, all the disciples were in deep sorrow. But they all got together to comfort one another—except for Thomas. John 20:24 says, "Thomas, called the Twin, one of the twelve, was not with them."

Thomas missed the whole thing.

Read John 20:19-24 in your Bible. What did Thomas miss by not being with the other apostles?

_____

Why wasn't Thomas there? _____

It's possible that Thomas was so negative, so pessimistic, such a melancholy person, that he was absolutely destroyed, and he was probably off somewhere wallowing in his own misery. He could see only the worst of everything. Now his worst fear had been realized. Jesus was gone, and Thomas was sure he would never see Him again. He may have still been thinking he would never find the way to get where Jesus was. He was no doubt regretting the fact that he did not die with Jesus, as he had been so determined to do in the first place.

Thomas may well have felt alone, betrayed, rejected, forsaken. It was over. The One he loved so deeply was gone, and it tore his heart out. He was not in a mood to socialize. He was brokenhearted, shattered, devastated, crushed. He just wanted to be alone. He simply couldn't take the banter. He wasn't in a mood to be in a crowd, even with his friends.

"The other disciples therefore said to him, 'We have seen the Lord'" (v. 25). They were exuberant. They were ecstatic. They were eager to share the good news with Thomas.

But someone in the kind of mood Thomas was in was not going to be cheered up so easily. He was still being a hopeless pessimist. All he could see was the bad side of things, and this was just too good to be true. "So he said to them, 'Unless I see in His hands the print of the nails, and put my finger into the print of the nails, and put my hand into His side, I will not believe'" (v. 25).

Because of that statement Thomas has been nicknamed "Doubting Thomas." _All_ the apostles were slow to believe (John 20:20). What set Thomas apart from the other ten was not that his doubt was greater but that his sorrow was greater.

John 20:26 says that eight days passed after Jesus appeared to the disciples. Finally Thomas's ragged grief apparently had eased a bit. Because this time Thomas was with the apostles when they returned to the room where Jesus appeared to them. Once again, "Jesus came, the doors being shut, and stood in the midst, and said, 'Peace to you!'" (v. 26).

Week of AUGUST 21

Read John 20:26-27 in your Bible. Check the statements that reflect what Jesus said to Thomas.
- ❏ "Shape up or ship out."
- ❏ "I'll meet you where you are."
- ❏ "There's no room for a Gloomy Gus in My kingdom."
- ❏ "There's no longer any reason for doubt or darkness. Believe!"

The Lord was amazingly gentle with him. Thomas had erred because he was more or less wired to be a pessimist. But it was the error of profound love. It was provoked by grief, brokenheartedness, uncertainty, and the pain of loneliness. No one could feel the way Thomas felt unless he loved Jesus the way Thomas loved Him. So Jesus was tender with him. He understands our weaknesses (Hebrews 4:15). So He understands our doubt. He sympathizes with our uncertainty. He is patient with our pessimism.

Then Thomas made what was probably the greatest statement ever to come from the lips of the apostles: "My Lord and my God!" (v. 28). Let those who question the deity of Christ meet Thomas!

Suddenly, Thomas's melancholy, comfortless, negative, moody tendencies were forever banished by the appearance of Jesus Christ. And in that moment he was transformed into a great evangelist. A short time later, at Pentecost, along with the other apostles, he was filled with the Holy Spirit and empowered for ministry. He, like his comrades, took the gospel to the ends of the earth.

A considerable amount of ancient testimony suggests that Thomas carried the gospel as far as India. The strongest traditions say he was martyred for his faith by being run through with a spear—a fitting form of martyrdom for one whose faith came of age when he saw the spear mark in his Master's side.

> "For we do not have a High Priest who cannot sympathize with our weaknesses, but was in all points tempted as we are, yet without sin" (Hebrews 4:15, NKJV).

How did your glimpse into Thomas's life:

Encourage you? _____

_____

Challenge you? _____

_____

Amy SUMMERS

leader Guide

NOTES

To the Leader:

Make contact with those learners who are heading up your class ministry project discussed in last week's session. Offer your support as they plan this ministry. Announce the time and date (if already established) at the beginning of your session and encourage all learners to be involved.

Before the Session

1. Fill a drinking glass half full with water. Place it in a low-lipped bowl. Have on hand a pitcher of water.

During the Session:

1. Ask: *When you joined in playground games as a child, were you usually the first person chosen for a team, the last, or somewhere in between? Describe how you felt as you waited for a team captain to call your name. How did you feel when you were finally chosen? Why?* Comment that the Apostle Thomas was such a pessimist that he probably thought he'd never be chosen for a team and assumed any team that chose him would lose anyway. The Apostle Matthew would never be chosen because everyone hated him. Jesus not only chose both of these men, He transformed them into victors. OR Display the glass (make sure it's in the bowl). Ask, *Are you the kind of person who'd say this glass is half empty, half full, or question whether the glass actually exists?* Allow volunteers to explain their responses. State that the Apostle Matthew was so hated that his own people would not have offered him a glass of water. Thomas was such a pessimist that he would have declared the glass was half empty or doubted its existence. However, these men's relationships with Jesus so transformed them that eventually their lives overflowed with love and service for Christ. As you make that last statement, pour water into the glass until it overflows.

2. Explain why Matthew was so hated by the Jews. Invite someone to read Luke 5:27-28. Discuss the first question in Day 2. Ask learners if they would rather attend a banquet with members of an organized crime family, IRS agents, or leaders of a religious organization. Have them state why. Direct learners to listen for which description best fits those who attended Matthew's banquet as you read Luke 5:29-30. Call for responses and allow volunteers to share why they chose that response. Discuss the first activity of Day 1. Invite someone to read Luke 5:31-32. Ask: *Did the Pharisees consider themselves spiritually*

Week of AUGUST 21

healthy or spiritually sick? Why? Did Matthew consider himself spiritually healthy or spiritually sick? What gives you that impression? Who received spiritual healing? Why?

3. Request volunteers read aloud Matthew 1:22; 2:17,23. Ask what clue this gives us about Matthew. [He knew the Old Testament.] Ask what else we know about Matthew (see second to last paragraph of Day 2). Direct learners to scan Matthew 2 in their Bibles and state who Matthew recorded as the first persons to worship Jesus. [Gentiles] Request a volunteer read Matthew 28:19. Ask: *Judging from the beginning and ending of his Gospel, who did Matthew declare could follow Christ? How did his own experience influence his message?* Discuss the final activity of Day 2.

4. Direct learners to think of their worst personality flaw. Ask them to silently consider: *How hard have I tried to get rid of this flaw? How successful have I been?* Comment that although Thomas is often known as "Doubting Thomas," he most likely struggled more with pessimism than doubt. Summarize the events described in John 10:22–11:15. Invite someone to read John 11:16. Discuss the second activity in Day 3, using Dr. MacArthur's comments to add to the discussion. Ask if natural pessimists have to become optimists before they can serve Christ and why. Ask why learners agree or disagree that heroic pessimism is real courage. Discuss both activities in Day 4.

5. Invite someone to read John 20:19-24. Ask why Thomas wasn't there for that meeting. (You may want to explore another possibility for Thomas' absence, such as, he was a man of great courage and perhaps he was the only apostle who wasn't hiding out in fear.) Request a volunteer read aloud John 20:25-28. Ask learners to imagine that they are movie directors shooting this scene: *Where will you focus the camera? What are the other disciples doing? What tone of voice will you direct the actor portraying Jesus to use with Thomas? What are Jesus' facial expressions? Does Thomas actually touch Jesus' hands and side? What actions does Thomas take? How is Thomas's character different after this encounter?*

6. Ask learners to suggest ways Jesus can transform naturally pessimistic persons. Discuss the final activity in Day 5. Close in prayer, thanking God for choosing outcasts and asking for power to believe Him regardless of the circumstances.

NOTES

THE LAST FOUR

day One

The final group of four apostles is the least known to us, except for Judas Iscariot, who made himself notorious by selling Christ to be crucified. This group seems to have been less intimate with Christ than the other eight disciples. They are virtually silent in the Gospel narratives. Little is known about any of them, except the fact that they were appointed to be apostles.

James the Less

The ninth name in Luke's list of the apostles (Luke 6:14–16) is "James the son of Alphaeus" (v. 15). The *only* thing Scripture tells us about this man is his name. If he ever wrote anything, it is lost to history. If he ever asked Jesus any questions or did anything to stand out from the group, Scripture does not record it. He never attained any degree of fame or notoriety. He was not the kind of person who stands out. He was utterly obscure. He even had a common name.

There are several men with the name *James* in the New Testament. We have already met James the son of Zebedee. There was another James, who was the son of Mary and Joseph and therefore a half brother of Christ (Galatians 1:19). The James who was Jesus' half brother became a leader in the Jerusalem church. He was the spokesman who delivered the ruling at the Jerusalem Council in Acts 15:13–21. He is also thought to be the same James who penned the New Testament epistle that bears his name. He is not the same James named as one of the apostles.

Practically all we know about the James is the names of his family members.

Read Mark 3:18 in your Bible and Mark 15:40 in the margin on page 153. Identify James's:

Week of AUGUST 28

Father: _____

Mother: _____

Brother: _____

> "There were also women looking on from afar, among whom were Mary Magdalene, Mary the mother of James the Less and of Joses, and Salome" (Mark 15:40, NKJV).

Joses must have been well-known as a follower of the Lord (though not an apostle) because his name is mentioned repeatedly. Their mother, Mary, was obviously a devoted follower of Christ as well. She was an eyewitness to the crucifixion. She is also one of the women who came to prepare Jesus' body for burial (Mark 16:1).

Aside from those scant details that can be gleaned about James's family, this James is utterly obscure. His lack of prominence is even reflected in his nickname.

In Mark 15:40 in the margin circle James's nickname.

The Greek word for "Less" is *mikros*. It literally means "little." Its primary meaning is "small in stature," so it could refer to his physical features. Perhaps he was a short or small-framed man.

The word can also speak of someone who is young in age. He might have been younger than James the son of Zebedee, so that this title would distinguish him as the younger of the two.

But the name most likely refers to his influence. James the son of Zebedee was a man of prominence. His family was known to the high priest (John 18:15–16). He was part of the Lord's most intimate inner circle. He was the better known of the two Jameses. Therefore, James the son of Alphaeus was known as "James the Less." *Mikros.* "Little James."

We might say James's distinguishing mark was his obscurity. That in itself is a significant fact. Apparently he sought no recognition. He displayed no great leadership. He asked no critical questions. He demonstrated no unusual insight. Only his name remains, while his life and his labors are immersed in obscurity. But he was one of the Twelve. The Lord selected him for a reason, trained and empowered him like the others, and sent him out as a witness.

Early church history is also mostly silent about this man named James. Some of the earliest legends about him confuse him with James the brother of the Lord. There is some evidence that James the Less took the gospel to

Syria and Persia. Accounts of his death differ. Some say he was stoned; others say he was beaten to death; still others say he was crucified like his Lord.

Simon the Zealot

The tenth name listed by Luke is "Simon called the Zealot" (Luke 6:15). In Matthew 10:4 and Mark 3:18 he is called "Simon the Cananite." That is not a reference to the land of Canaan or the village of Cana. It comes from the Hebrew root *qanna*, which means "to be zealous."

Simon was apparently at one time a member of the political party known as the Zealots. The fact that he bore the title all his life may also suggest that he had a fiery, zealous temperament. But the term *Zealot* in Jesus' day signified a well-known and widely feared outlaw political sect, and Simon had apparently been a member of that sect.

The Zealots hated the Romans, and their goal was to overthrow the Roman occupation. They advanced their agenda primarily through terrorism and surreptitious acts of violence.

The Zealots were hoping for a Messiah who would lead them in overthrowing the Romans and restore the kingdom to Israel with its Solomonic glory. They were red-hot patriots, ready to die in an instant for what they believed in. Simon was one of them.

As one of the Twelve, Simon had to associate with Matthew, who was at the opposite end of the political spectrum, collecting taxes for the Roman government. At one point in his life, Simon probably would have gladly killed Matthew. In the end, they became spiritual brethren, working side by side for the same cause—the spread of the gospel—and worshiping the same Lord.

"A new commandment I give to you, that you love one another; as I have loved you, that you also love one another. By this all will know that you are My disciples, if you have love for one another" (John 13:34-35, NKJV).

Read John 13:34-35 in the margin. How would a loving relationship between Simon the Zealot and Matthew the tax collector be a strong witness to the power of Christ?

Week of AUGUST 28

It's amazing Jesus would select a man like Simon to be an apostle. But he was a man of fierce loyalties, amazing passion, courage, and zeal. Simon had believed the truth and embraced Christ as his Lord. The fiery enthusiasm he once had for Israel was now expressed in his devotion to Christ.

Several early sources say that after the destruction of Jerusalem, Simon took the gospel north and preached in the British Isles. Like so many of the others, Simon simply disappears from the biblical record. There is no reliable record of what happened to him, but all accounts say he was killed for preaching the gospel. This man who was once willing to kill and be killed for a political agenda within the confines of Judea found a more fruitful cause for which to give his life—in the proclamation of salvation for sinners out of every nation, tongue, and tribe.

day Three

Judas: Apostle with Three Names

The last name on the list of faithful disciples is "Judas, the son of James" (Luke 6:16). The name *Judas* in and of itself is a fine name. It means "Jehovah leads." But because of the treachery of Judas Iscariot, the name *Judas* will forever bear a negative connotation. When the Apostle John mentions this Judas, he calls him "Judas (not Iscariot)" (John 14:22).

Judas the son of James actually had three names. Jerome, the great church father, referred to him as "Trinomious"—the man with three names. In Matthew 10:3 he is called "Lebbaeus, whose surname was Thaddaeus." *Judas* was probably the name given him at birth. *Lebbaeus* and *Thaddaeus* were essentially nicknames. *Thaddaeus* means "breast child"—evoking the idea of a nursing baby. It almost has a derisive sound, like "mamma's boy." Perhaps he was the youngest in his family, and therefore the baby among several siblings—specially cherished by his mother. His other name, *Lebbaeus,* is similar. It is from a Hebrew root that refers to the heart—literally, "heart child."

Both names suggest he had a tender, childlike heart. It is interesting to think of such a gentle soul hanging around in the same subgroup of four apostles as Simon the Zealot. But the Lord can use both kinds. Zealots make great preachers. But so do tender-hearted, compassionate, gentle, sweet-spirited souls like Lebbaeus Thaddaeus.

The New Testament records one incident involving this Judas Lebbaeus Thaddaeus. To see it, we turn to the Apostle John's description of Jesus' Upper-Room Discourse.

Read John 14:21-22 in your Bible. What does Judas's question reveal about his character?

_____

Here we see the tender-hearted humility of this man. He doesn't say anything brash or bold or overconfident. He doesn't rebuke the Lord like Peter once did. His question is full of gentleness and meekness and devoid of any sort of pride. He couldn't believe that Jesus would manifest Himself to this rag-tag group of eleven and not to the whole world. After all, Jesus was the Savior of the world. The good news of forgiveness and salvation was certainly good news for all the world. But the rest of the world was still, by and large, clueless. So Lebbaeus Thaddaeus wanted to know, "Why are you going to disclose Yourself to us and not to the whole world?"

Jesus gave him a marvelous answer, and the answer was as tender as the question. "Jesus answered and said to him, 'If anyone loves Me, he will keep My word; and My Father will love him, and We will come to him and make Our home with him'" (John 14:23). In other words, Christ will manifest Himself to anyone who loves Him.

Most of the early tradition regarding Lebbaeus Thaddaeus suggests that a few years after Pentecost he took the gospel north, to Edessa, a royal city in Mesopotamia, in the region of Turkey today. There are numerous ancient accounts of how he healed the king of Edessa, a man named Abgar. In the fourth century, Eusebius the church historian said the archives at Edessa (now destroyed) contained full records of Thaddaeus's visit and the healing of Abgar.

The traditional apostolic symbol of Judas Lebbaeus Thaddaeus is a club, because tradition says he was clubbed to death for his faith.

If you desire to dig deeper...

Compare the lists of apostles in Matthew 10:2-4; Mark 3:16-19; Luke 6:13-16; and Acts 1:13.

Write the apostles' names below. Circle the names (besides Judas Iscariot) that don't appear in every list. What conclusion do you draw from your comparison?

1. _____
2. _____
3. _____
4. _____
5. _____
6. _____
7. _____
8. _____
9. _____
10. _____
11. _____
12. _____
13. _____

Week of **AUGUST 28**

How did your study of these three apostles:

Encourage you? _____

_____

Challenge you? _____

_____

Judas—The Traitor

The most notorious and universally scorned of all the disciples is Judas Iscariot, the betrayer. His name appears last in every biblical list of apostles except for the list in Acts 1, where it doesn't appear at all. Every time Judas is mentioned in Scripture, we also find a notation about his being a traitor. He is the most colossal failure in all of human history. He committed the most horrible, heinous act of any individual, ever. He betrayed the perfect, sinless, holy Son of God for a handful of money. His dark story is a poignant example of the depths to which the human heart is capable of sinking. He spent years with Jesus Christ, but for all that time his heart was only growing hard and hateful.

The other eleven apostles are all great encouragements to us because they exemplify how common people with typical failings can be used by God in *un*common, remarkable ways. Judas, on the other hand, stands as a warning about the evil potential of spiritual carelessness, squandered opportunity, sinful lusts, and hardness of the heart. Here was a man who drew as close to the Savior as it is humanly possible to be. He enjoyed every privilege Christ affords. He was intimately familiar with everything Jesus taught. Yet he remained in unbelief and went into a hopeless eternity.

Judas was as common as the rest, without earthly credentials and without any characteristics that made him stand out from the group. He began exactly like the others had begun. But he never laid hold of the truth by faith, so he was never transformed like the rest. While they were increasing in faith as sons of God, he was becoming more and more a child of hell.

The New Testament tells us plenty about Judas—enough to accomplish two things: First, the life of Judas reminds us that it is possible to be near Christ and associate with Him closely (but superficially) and yet become utterly hardened in sin. Second, Judas reminds us that no matter how sinful a person may be, no matter what treachery he or she may attempt against God, the purpose of God cannot be thwarted. Even the worst act of treachery works toward the fulfillment of the divine plan. God's sovereign plan cannot be overthrown even by the most cunning schemes of those who hate Him.

JUDAS'S NAME

Judas's name is a form of *Judah*. The name means "Jehovah leads," which indicates that when he was born his parents must have had great hopes for him to be led by God. The irony of the name is that no individual was ever more clearly led by Satan than Judas was.

His surname, *Iscariot*, signifies the region he came from. It is derived from the Hebrew term *ish* ("man") and the name of a town, Kerioth—"man of Kerioth." Judas probably came from Kerioth-hezron (see Joshua 15:25), a humble town in the south of Judea. He was apparently the only one of the apostles who did not come from Galilee.

Judas's father was named Simon (John 6:71). This Simon is otherwise unknown to us.

> "Jesus answered them, 'Did I not choose you, the twelve, and one of you is a devil?' He spoke of Judas Iscariot, the son of Simon, for it was he who would betray Him, being one of the twelve"
> (John 6:70-71, NKJV).

JUDAS'S CALL

The call of Judas is not recorded in Scripture. It is obvious, however, that he followed Jesus willingly. Scripture does say that when Jesus chose Judas as one of His apostles, He *knew* Judas would be the one to fulfill the prophecies of betrayal. Jesus knowingly chose him to fulfill the plan.

JUDAS'S DISILLUSIONMENT

The few glimpses of Judas that are shown to us from time to time in the Gospels suggest that he had long been growing progressively more disillusioned and embittered but kept it hidden from everyone. As early as John 6:70, during Jesus' Galilean ministry, Jesus referred to Judas as "a devil." Jesus knew what no one else knew: Judas was becoming disgruntled

Week of AUGUST 28

already. He was still unbelieving, unrepentant, and unregenerate; and he was growing more and more hardhearted all the time.

By the time Jesus and the apostles went to Jerusalem for the Passover in the last year of Jesus' earthly ministry, Judas's spiritual disenfranchisement was complete. At some point in those final few days, his disillusionment turned to hate, and hate mixed with greed finally turned to treachery.

JUDAS'S AVARICE

Shortly after the raising of Lazarus and just before Jesus' triumphal entry into Jerusalem, Jesus and the disciples returned to Bethany, on the outskirts of the city. This was the place Lazarus and his sisters Mary and Martha lived. Jesus was invited to a meal at the home of one "Simon the Leper" (Matthew 26:6). His dear friend Lazarus was present with Mary and Martha, who were helping serve the meal. Read what John 12:2–3 records happened.

This act was shocking in its extravagance. It had the appearance of wastefulness. Obviously perfume—especially such an expensive fragrance—is designed to be used in small amounts. Once poured out, it cannot be reused. To pour out a pound of expensive oil and use it to anoint someone's feet gave the appearance of gross excess.

Judas's response was a clever ploy. He feigned concern for the poor. "Then one of His disciples, Judas Iscariot, Simon's son, who would betray Him, said, 'Why was this fragrant oil not sold for three hundred denarii and given to the poor?'" (vv. 4–5). Three hundred denarii was a lot of money for perfume by any measure. Remember, a denarius was basically a working man's daily wage (Matthew 20:2). Three hundred denarii is a full year's wages (allowing for Sabbaths and holidays off).

Apparently Judas's protest seemed reasonable to the other apostles too because Matthew 26:8 says they all echoed Judas's indignation. What an expert Judas had become in his hypocrisy!

Read John 12:6 in your Bible. Who was Judas really concerned about? (circle one)

The poor   The disciples   Jesus   Himself

Of course, neither John nor any of the other apostles saw through Judas's deceit at the time, but in retrospect, and writing his book under the Holy Spirit's inspiration, John told us plainly what Judas's motive was: sheer greed. Three hundred denarii would have been a lot to add to the treasury, offering a prime opportunity for Judas to skim money for his own pocket. Because of Jesus' willingness to receive such lavish worship, Judas missed a prime opportunity to embezzle funds.

Jesus' gentle reprimand in John 12:7–8 seems to have made Judas resent Jesus even more. Judas did not repent. He did not even examine his own heart.

Read Matthew 26:6-16 in your Bible.
How was this incident a turning point for Judas? _____

Judas crept away, left Bethany, walked about a mile and a half to Jerusalem, met with the chief priests, and sold Jesus to His enemies for a pocketful of coins. Thirty pieces of silver. That is all he could get. According to Exodus 21:32, it was the price of a slave. It was not much money, but it was all he could negotiate.

Notice that this is the first time Judas had ever exposed himself in any way. Up to that point, he had blended in perfectly with the rest of the group. This is the first time on record that he spoke out as an individual, and it is the first time he merited any kind of direct rebuke from Christ. Apparently, that is all that was needed to provoke his betrayal. He had kept his bitterness and disillusionment bottled up as long as he could. Now it spilled forth in secret treachery.

Are you harboring secret resentment or disillusionment in your heart? _____
How is this resentment hurting yourself or those you love? _____
What steps will you take to let go of those resentments? _____

Consider speaking with your pastor or Bible study leader for counsel and encouragement.

Week of AUGUST 28

The Son of Perdition

JUDAS'S HYPOCRISY

John 13:1 begins the apostle John's lengthy account of what happened in the Upper Room on the night of Jesus' arrest. Having already taken money to betray Christ, Judas came back, blended into the group, and pretended nothing unusual had happened. John says it was the Devil who put it in the heart of Judas to betray Jesus (v. 2). Satan could not *force* Judas to betray Jesus. But Satan through some means suggested the plot, tempted Judas to do this thing, and planted the very seed of treachery in his heart. Judas's heart was so hostile to the truth and so filled with evil that Judas became a willing instrument of Satan himself.

It was at this very point that Jesus gave the apostles a lesson in humility by washing their feet. He washed the feet of all twelve, which means He even washed the feet of Judas. Judas sat there and let Jesus wash his feet and remained utterly unmoved. The world's worst sinner was also the world's best hypocrite.

When Peter protested Jesus' action, Jesus replied, "He who is bathed needs only to wash his feet, but is completely clean; and you are clean, *but not all of you*" (v. 10, emphasis added). A buzz must have gone around the room when Jesus said that. There were only twelve of them, and Jesus was saying that someone in the group was not clean. John adds, "For He knew who would betray Him; therefore He said, 'You are not all clean'" (v. 11).

In verses 18–19 Jesus spoke even more directly: "I do not speak concerning all of you. I know whom I have chosen; but that the Scripture may be fulfilled, 'He who eats bread with Me has lifted up his heel against Me.' Now I tell you before it comes, that when it does come to pass, you may believe that I am He."

All of that, however, seems to have gone over the heads of most of the apostles. So in verse 21, Jesus makes an even more explicit prediction about the impending act of betrayal: "When Jesus had said these things, He was troubled in spirit, and testified and said, 'Most assuredly, I say to

If you desire to dig deeper...

Read Romans 6:12-14.

State ways you can offer a specific part of your body to sin as an instrument of wickedness. Identify possible results of that evil behavior.

Now state ways you can offer that same body part to God as an instrument of righteousness. Identify possible results of that godly action.

you, one of you will betray Me.'" All the disciples except Judas were perplexed and deeply troubled by this. They apparently began to examine their own hearts, because Matthew 26:22 says, "They were exceedingly sorrowful, and each of them began to say to Him, 'Lord, is it I?'" Even Judas, ever careful to keep up the appearance of being like everyone else, asked, "Rabbi, is it I?" (v. 25). Judas asked the question only because he was worried about how the others perceived him; he already knew that he was the one of whom Jesus spoke.

**Read John 13:21-30 in your Bible.
On a scale of 1 to 10, with 1 being not at all, how explicit was Jesus in identifying His betrayer?**

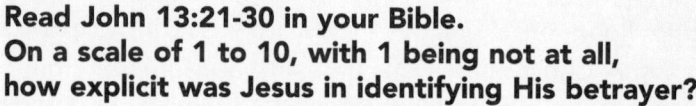

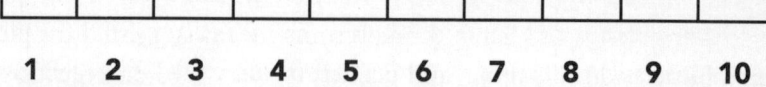

In your opinion, why didn't the apostles then understand that Judas was the traitor?

_____

Only after Judas had left did our Lord institute the Lord's Supper.

JUDAS'S BETRAYAL

Judas apparently went straight from the Upper Room to the Sanhedrin. He reported to them that the final breach had been made, and he now knew where they could apprehend Jesus under cover of darkness. Judas had been secretly seeking a convenient opportunity to betray Jesus ever since making his bargain with the Sanhedrin (Mark 14:11). Now the time had come.

Read Luke 22:3-6 in the margin. Underline the conditions Judas had been waiting for to carry out his betrayal.

What does this say to you about Judas's character?

_____

"Then Satan entered Judas, called Iscariot, one of the Twelve. And Judas went to the chief priests and the officers of the temple guard and discussed with them how he might betray Jesus. They were delighted and agreed to give him money. He consented, and watched for an opportunity to hand Jesus over to them when no crowd was present" (Luke 22:3-6, NKJV).

Week of AUGUST 28

Judas was a coward. He knew the popularity of Jesus. He was afraid of the crowd.

Judas knew Jesus regularly went to Gethsemane to pray with His disciples (Luke 22:39; John 18:2). So Judas knew exactly where to bring the authorities to capture Jesus.

In John 18, Judas's conspiracy of betrayal reaches its culmination. "Then Judas, having received a detachment of troops, and officers from the chief priests and Pharisees, came there with lanterns, torches, and weapons" (v. 3). The "detachment of troops" was most likely a Roman cohort from the Antonio Fortress, adjacent to the temple. A full cohort numbered about six hundred men. No exact figure is given, but all the Gospel writers say it was a great multitude (Matthew 26:47; Mark 14:43; Luke 22:47)—probably hundreds of soldiers. They obviously expected the worst. They came armed to the teeth.

"Jesus therefore, knowing all things that would come upon Him, went forward and said to them, 'Whom are you seeking?'" (John 18:4). Jesus did not wait for Judas to single Him out; He did not try to hide; He "went forward," presenting Himself to them, and said, "I am He" (v. 5).

Judas had a prearranged signal to identify Jesus: "Whomever I kiss, He is the One; seize Him" (Matthew 26:48). What a diabolical way to point out Jesus! But his wretchedness was so profound and his hypocrisy so malicious that he seemingly had no conscience. Furthermore, since Jesus stepped forward and identified Himself, the signal would have been unnecessary, but Judas—cynic and scoundrel that he had become—kissed Jesus anyway (Mark 14:45).

"Jesus said to him, 'Judas, are you betraying the Son of Man with a kiss?'" (Luke 22:48). Kissing is a mark of homage, love, affection, tenderness, respect, and intimacy. Judas's feigned feelings for Christ only made his deed that much darker. It was a devious hypocrisy, trying to keep up the veneer of respect even to the bitter end.

Jesus, ever gracious, even addressed Judas as "Friend" (Matthew 26:50). But Judas was no true friend of Jesus (see John 15:14). He was a betrayer and a deceiver. His kisses were the kisses of the worst kind of treachery.

Would you be able to call your enemy and betrayer a "friend"? ❑ Yes ❑ No

JUDAS'S DEATH

Judas sold Jesus for a pittance. But as soon as the deal was complete, Judas's conscience immediately came alive. He found himself in a hell of his own making, hammered by his own mind for what he had done. The money, which had been so important to him before, now did not matter. Matthew 27:3–4 says, "Then Judas, His betrayer, seeing that He had been condemned, was remorseful and brought back the thirty pieces of silver to the chief priests and elders, saying, 'I have sinned by betraying innocent blood.'"

Judas's remorse was not the same as repentance, as subsequent events clearly show. He was sorry, not because he had sinned against Christ, but because his sin did not satisfy him the way he had hoped.

The chief priests and elders were unsympathetic. "They said, 'What is that to us? You see to it!'" (v. 4). They had what they wanted. Judas could do what he liked with the money. Nothing would undo his treachery now.

Matthew says, "Then he threw down the pieces of silver in the temple and departed, and went and hanged himself" (v. 5). Judas was already in a hell of his own making. His conscience would not be silenced. Sin brings guilt, and Judas's sin brought him unbearable misery. Again, his remorse was not genuine repentance. If that were the case, he would not have killed himself. He was merely sorry because he did not like what he felt.

Sadly, Judas did not seek the forgiveness of God. He did not cry out for mercy. He did not seek deliverance from Satan. Instead, he tried to silence his conscience by killing himself.

Acts 1:18–19 adds a final note to the tragedy of Judas, with more detail about his death and the acquisition of the Field of Blood. Apparently he chose a tree on an overhang above some jagged rocks to hang himself. Either the rope or the tree branch broke, and Judas fell headlong onto the rocks. The biblical description is graphic and ugly: "He burst open in the middle and all his entrails gushed out" (Acts 1:18). Judas was such a tragic figure that he couldn't even kill himself the way he wanted to.

This is virtually the last word in Scripture about Judas: "His entrails gushed out." His life and his death were grotesque tragedies. He was a child of hell and a son of perdition (John 17:12), and he went to his own place where he belonged (Acts 1:25).

Week of AUGUST 28

Read Mark 14:21 in your Bible. What chilling statement did Jesus make about Judas?

_____

THE MORAL OF JUDAS'S LIFE

We can draw some important lessons from the life of Judas.

First, Judas is a tragic example of lost opportunity. He heard Jesus teach day in and day out for several years. He could have asked Jesus any question he liked. He could have sought and received from the Lord any help he needed. He could have exchanged the oppressive burden of his sin for an easy yoke. Yet in the end Judas was damned because of his own failure to heed what he heard.

Second, Judas is the epitome of wasted privilege. He was given the highest place of privilege among all the Lord's followers, but he squandered that privilege—cashed it in for a fistful of coins he decided he did not really want after all. What a stupid bargain!

Third, Judas is the classic illustration of how the love of money is a root of all kinds of evil (1 Timothy 6:10).

Fourth, Judas exemplifies the ugliness and danger of spiritual betrayal. Would that Judas were the only hypocrite who ever betrayed the Lord, but that is not so. There are Judases in every age—people who seem to be true disciples and close followers of Christ but who turn against Him for sinister and selfish reasons.

Fifth, Judas is proof of the patient, forbearing goodness and loving-kindness of Christ. Jesus even showed His loving-kindness to a reprobate like Judas. Remember, Jesus was still calling him "Friend," even in the midst of Judas's betrayal. Jesus never showed Judas anything but kindness and charity, even though the Lord knew all along what Judas was planning to do.

Sixth, Judas demonstrates how the sovereign will of God cannot be thwarted by any means. His betrayal of Christ seemed at first glance like Satan's greatest triumph ever. But in reality, it signaled utter defeat for the Devil and all his works (Hebrews 2:14; 1 John 3:8).

Seventh, Judas is a vivid demonstration of the deceitfulness and fruitlessness of hypocrisy. Judas was so expert at his hypocrisy that none of the other eleven ever suspected him. But he could never fool Jesus. Nor can any hypocrite.

> "He who sins is of the devil, for the devil has sinned from the beginning. For this purpose the Son of God was manifested, that He might destroy the works of the devil" (1 John 3:8, NKJV).

John MacARTHUR

If you have enjoyed these studies from John MacArthur and desire to purchase your own copy of his book Twelve Ordinary Men *(ISBN: 0-8499-1773-5) to read and study in greater detail, visit the LifeWay Christian Store serving you. Or you can order a copy by calling 1-800-233-1123.*

When Judas bartered away the life of Christ, he was in effect selling his own soul to the Devil. The tragedy of his life was a tragedy of his own making. He ignored the light he had been exposed to for all those years, and thus he relegated himself to eternal darkness.

After Jesus' resurrection, Judas's apostolic office was filled by Matthias (Acts 1:16–26). The Apostle Peter said, "For it is written in the Book of Psalms: 'Let his dwelling place be desolate, and let no one live in it'; and, 'Let another take his office'" (v. 20). Matthias was selected because he had been with Jesus and the other apostles "from the baptism of John to that day when He was taken up from us" (v. 22). Nothing is known of Matthias other than that. His name appears only twice in Scripture, both times in Acts 1 in the account of how he was chosen. Thus in the end, another perfectly ordinary man was chosen. Along with the other eleven, Matthias became a powerful witness of Jesus' resurrection—one more ordinary man whom the Lord elevated to an extraordinary calling.

How did your study of Judas Iscariot serve as a:

Warning? _____

_____

Challenge? _____

_____

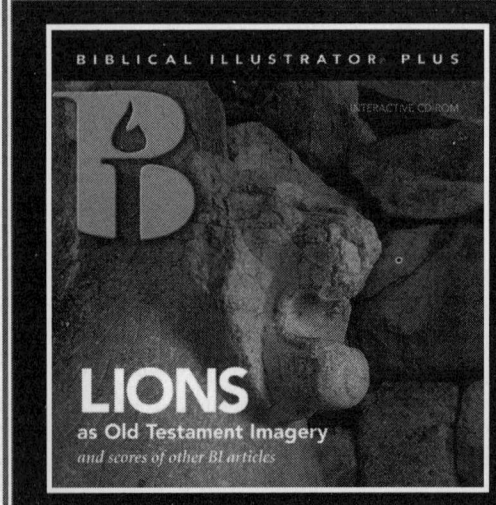

Look for articles that support MasterWork *in Biblical Illustrator Plus beginning in Fall 2005. Place your order for BI Plus, an interactive CD-ROM, on the Dated Literature Order Form or see your minister of education or Sunday School director.*

Week of AUGUST 28

Before the Session
1. Make six placards: 1. Lost Opportunity; 2. Wasted Privilege; 3. Danger of Spiritual Betrayal; 4. Patience and Love of Christ; 5. Sovereignty of God; 6. Fruitlessness of Hypocrisy. Display these when directed in Steps 4-7. (Option—write these headings on the board as you discuss each topic.)

During the Session
1. Ask learners if they would rather be famous, infamous, or unknown and why. Discuss why a person would choose notoriety over a good reputation. Comment that you have studied the better-known apostles. Today you will look at three relatively unknown apostles and the one apostle who chose to go down in infamy. OR Ask what each of the following groups of people have in common: Billy Graham, Jonathan Edwards, Billy Sunday [famous evangelists]; James the Less, Thaddeus, Simon the Zealot [apostles of Christ]; Mary Magdalene, Mary the mother of James, Salome [went to Jesus' tomb to anoint His body]; Benedict Arnold, Julius and Ethel Rosenberg, Judas Iscariot [traitors]. Remark that this study will challenge learners to be listed with the faithful rather than with the traitors.
2. Discuss the first activity of Day 1. Ask: *Do you think James was an apostle because his family was dedicated to Christ or did his family become dedicated to Christ through his influence? Give a reason for your opinion.* Discuss how learners can influence their families to be committed to Christ. Ask the class to identify James's nickname. Ask, *How is "Less" more when it refers to people who choose to serve Christ in obscurity?*
3. Discuss the activities about Simon and Thaddeus in Days 2 and 3. Ask: *Which of the three apostles in Days 1-3 reminds you of someone you know? Which reminds you of yourself? What does this say to you about whom Jesus chooses to serve Him?* Discuss the final activity of Day 3.
4. Explain the irony of the name *Judas*. Comment that believers must take a hard look at this wasted life so they can learn valuable lessons about

NOTES

To the Leader:

Depending on the amount of class time available, leaders may choose to introduce the first three apostles in this week's lesson briefly and then spend most of the lesson time on Judas the betrayer.

Visit prospects and chronic absentees this week. Take them a Fall issue of *MasterWork* and invite them to join your Bible study group as you begin a study of the life and ministry of the Apostle Paul by Beth Moore.

167

themselves and God. Display the first placard. Invite volunteers to recall some of the amazing things the apostles heard Jesus say and saw Him do. (Or direct learners who have Bibles with headings to skim the Gospel of Mark and state amazing things the apostles witnessed.) Inquire: *Judas had so many opportunities to place his complete faith in Jesus. Why didn't he?* Explore examples (without naming specific names) of how people today have the opportunity to witness the power and love of Jesus yet they still refuse to commit their lives to Him.

5. Display the second placard. Request someone read aloud John 12:1-6. Ask what privilege Judas had. Discuss how he could have used this privilege to have benefited God's kingdom. Invite someone to read Matthew 27:3-5. Ask what Judas traded his great privilege for and what the result was of that trade off. Explore how people today trade the privileges God gives them for worldly things and how that waste eventually leads to the ultimate fate Judas experienced.

6. Display the third placard. Invite someone to read Matthew 26:6-16. Ask how it is possible to be with Jesus and yet be so hardened by sin. From Day 4 discuss the danger of harboring resentment and bitterness. Display the fourth placard. Invite a volunteer to read John 13:1-11. Ask how Jesus could possibly wash the feet of the man He knew would betray Him. (Hint: the secret is in verse 3.) Request someone read Matthew 26:48-50. Inquire: *What amazes you about Jesus? How does this episode convict and encourage you?*

7. Display the fifth placard. Direct learners to read the paragraph in Day 4 that begins "The New Testament tells us plenty about Judas...." Ask them to state the bad news and the good news in the account of Judas. Display the final placard. Comment that hypocrites may fool everyone else, but they can never fool Jesus. Request someone read John 2:24-25. Urge learners to be certain that their hearts are clean before God—explain the steps to becoming a Christian on the inside front cover of this publication.

8. Discuss the final activity of Day 5. Invite volunteers to share what they have gained from this study of the twelve apostles. Close in prayer, asking God that learners will, like the apostles, be examples of faithful service to Christ.